SOMETIMES I FEEL LIKE A FATHERLESS CHILD

Sometimes I Feel Like a Fatherless Child
Copyright © 2013 by Noel Myricks

Seaburn Publishing Group
P.O. Box 2085
Long Island City NY 11102
www.seaburnbooks.com

Myricks, N
Sometimes I Feel Like a Fatherless Child
p. cm.
ISBN: 1-59232-411-8 Paperback
HHS061375H13 2013
617'.14_NY13   13-119254
CIP
Printed in the United States of America
10 9 7 5 4 3 2 1

SOMETIMES I FEEL LIKE A FATHERLESS CHILD

Noel Myricks, J.D., Ed.D

CONTENTS

FROM NEGRO TO BECOMING A BLACK MAN 212

SAN FRANCISCO – AND THE STRUGGLE TO BE 220

RETIREMENT 287

CONCLUSION 292

Noel Myricks

DEDICATION

This book is dedicated to the memory of James Baldwin, a giant of literature and racial critic, whose words, *"Writing was telling as much truth as you can bear"* was a source of inspiration for this book.

The subject is myself and the world. It required every ounce of stamina to look at myself and the world as I envisioned it during my journey through this life. Several years have passed since I first began writing this book. Now as I come close to the end of my life, I felt the need to make an effort to look back—reflect and meditate on it to make, to the extent possible, some meaning out of it.

All the names in the book with the exception of deceased persons, public figures and a few personal exceptions, and the author are entirely fictitious*, and any resemblance to the names of living persons is wholly coincidental.

INTRODUCTION

This book, *"Sometimes I Feel like a Fatherless Child"* is about an African-American male who was born out-of-wedlock in the welfare ward of Cook County hospital in Chicago, Ill., during the throes of the great depression. Within a year of his birth, his mother married, became pregnant again, had a miscarriage, was denied admission to a "whites only" hospital in Alabama while visiting relatives, and died there at the age of 22. It is a story about being raised in a suburb of Detroit in an extended family dominated primarily by women, the values inculcated and his struggles as a man child, and how he avoided the expectation of a teacher that he would either be dead or in Jackson Penitentiary before he graduated from high school.

The author describes various life experiences and how he periodically found himself one step from disaster. He describes how he came to the slow realization that every decision made has consequences, and how they can greatly influence the direction of one's life and negatively impact other lives even though not foreseen at the time. There are compelling reasons why we need to learn to make good decisions. It was only near the end of his life that the author came to the realization that the decisions we make should honor God. If this is done, it will not permit fear or a desire for acceptance to cause a person to behave in a way that conflicts with a Bible-trained conscience. Nor will it cause suffering to oneself and to others.

He also describes how major changes in his environment impacted on his personality, values and ideology, and the psychological metamorphosis that he experienced during his military service in the U.S. Navy, his college and professional experiences, and how he eventually experienced a spiritual metamorphosis as he approached the end of his life. And finally, how he realized the truth of King Solomon's words that "Everything is vanity." (Ecc. 3:19).

BIRTH AND EARLY CHILDHOOD

If the U.S. Supreme Court decision of *Roe v. Wade*, which gave women the constitutional right to have an abortion, had been the law of the land in 1935, the odds are substantial that I would not be writing this book today.

My Mother

My life began on a December day in *Cook County Hospital* on the south side of Chicago. My mother had come here, using a fictitious name and without the knowledge of her relatives so as to avoid embarrassing them to give birth to me. I was being born out-of-wedlock. As a child, I never knew my biological father, *Cliff Williams*. As an adult en route to law school, I returned briefly to my hometown to locate him. Eventually, at the age of 31, I located him and asked why he did not marry my mother or show any interest in me when I was a child.

My maternal relatives had always feigned ignorance as to their knowledge of the identity of my natural father. I had always been known as *Noel Myricks*, and had no reason to assume that I had another name at birth, or that *Wyman Myricks*, my step-father, was not my biological father. However, when I reached the age when child support payments from the welfare department stopped, a Social Worker came to my house and delivered my birth certificate to my aunt. Inquisitive as ever, I quickly retrieved it from her and saw a name that I did not recognize. Initially, I thought a mistake had been made by the Social Worker; a case of mistaken identity, but was assured that was my actual birth certificate.

Upon further inquiry from my aunt, all she could tell me was that she had no knowledge of the identity of my actual father because my mother was very secretive. Years later when I inquired again, she suggested that I contact *Chappie*, my uncle's wife who she described as being a very close confidant of my mother. We had not seen each other for at least 15 year

My Father

After a warm embrace and an exchange of greetings with Aunt Chappie, to my amazement when I inquired about the identity of my father, she looked at me and said, "Your mother told me that one day you would come and ask me this question." She inquired why I wanted to know who he was. I said that since I never knew my mother I would like to know who my father was before either of us died. She paused briefly and said, "His name is Cliff Williams." I did not recognize the name. And when I asked where I could find him, she told me where she thought he worked. I left immediately to locate him.

I went to a car wash in Detroit where I was told he might work and inquired of an attractive, seductive-looking female if she knew him. She smiled as though she had an intimate knowledge of him and said, "Yes, I know him. He does not work here; he works at the next car wash down the road."

I smiled and thanked her and proceeded to the next car wash. When I arrived I saw a man that I recognized as one of the persons who would attend my Aunt Georgia's card parties that she often had on weekends. As I looked closer, I noticed that his eyes, a very distinct light brown, were identical to my own. I immediately asked whether he was Cliff Williams?

He paused, looked at me and said, "It depends on who wants to know."

I smiled at his response and said somewhat haltingly, "My name is Noel Myricks. I have reason to believe that you may be my father."

Without blinking he said, "Well, who is your mother?"

I laughed and said, "Mollie—*Mollie Palmer*."

At that point he said, "I think there is a good possibility that I could be your father. We can't talk here. Can you come to my house this evening?"

I said sure.

He provided me with his address and then he asked whether I was married and I told him that I was and that I had a son. He asked me to bring them with me. When we arrived at his house in Southwest Detroit, to my surprise he told me, "I would like for you to meet the rest of your family."

He introduced me to his two daughters as their *brother*. They were cordial, but not particularly friendly. I recognized both of them as persons who had attended the same high school. We shook hands and they immediately left the room. After a few preliminary comments about my family and what I was doing with my life. I inquired about his relationship with my mother and why he had not been involved in my life. He said that he was "as helpful as he could be under the circumstances when she got pregnant." He had been a Numbers-man and was married at the time he seduced my mother and her father had threatened to kill him if he ever came around again, so he wisely kept away.

We spent approximately two hours together and my conversation with him had been beneficial. He had filled in an important gap in my life. He appeared to enjoy our conversation and delighted at the fact that I planned to become a lawyer. I told him that I would keep in touch. It was not long after I got out of law school that he died without the two of us ever talking again. I found out about his death through one of my boyhood friends.

When I returned to my hometown in *River Rouge, Michigan* some time later to attend the funeral of one of my relatives, I went by a doctor's office to say hello to one of his daughters who worked there as a receptionist. She was one of the two he had introduced me to when I came by his house.

I greeted her with a smile and said, "Hi! I'm your brother; thought I'd drop by and say hello while I was in town."

She gave me cold stare and said, "I have no brothers."

I looked at her and said, "I understand" and walked away.

We never saw each other again.

Within two months and 14 days after my birth, my mother would marry *Wyman Myricks* in *Toledo, Ohio* and I would become Noel Myricks. Within nine months and seven days after my birth, my mother would die while visiting relatives in Alabama for a family reunion. I would be raised by maternal grandparents. My grandfather died when I was four years old, and my grandmother died when I was 15 years old. After her death, I lived with two maternal aunts; one very briefly, and the other until such time that I graduated from high school and joined the navy.

My mother, Mollie, was the youngest and most adventuress of nine children. She had been the only one of nine children to graduate from high school. I would get to know her vicariously through memories that family members, friends and a former teacher had shared with me. Her trip to Alabama with some relatives and friends was supposed to be a joyous occasion. She would be attending what family members called, the *Big Meeting.* Today, we simply call it a family reunion.

Old acquaintances would be renewed with friends and family members who had been left behind when *Noah Palmer*, my grandfather, took his immediate family and moved north to seek greater opportunities than what was available to a black man in the south in the 1920's.

The trip back to the south was by automobile. It was long, hot and arduous. There were none of the amenities that so many of us take for granted today, such as air conditioned automobiles, easy access to quality hotels and motels.

Upon arriving in and around *Crenshaw County, Alabama*, my mother became ill from the afterbirth left in her from a miscarriage. The hospitals were reserved for *whites only*. She was assisted initially by a midwife and eventually a white doctor. She died at 22 years of age. Her body was returned to Michigan where she was buried in Woodmere Cemetery.

Now, at less than a year old, I began my life in the care and custody of my maternal grandmother and grandfather, and a strong support system of aunts, with minimal assistance from my uncles. My stepfather, the man whose surname I had, moved on and started a new life with another family and I rarely saw him during the remainder of his life. When he did make an occasional visit, he was always cordial and pleasant, but that was the extent of our contact and communication with each other.

His relatives in my community got irritated with me because I did not attend his funeral. Unfortunately, I did not know he had died until long after the fact. Even if I had known, I cannot be certain that I would have traveled from out of state to attend it since he had never been involved in my life. It's something I ponder to this day.

Parental Influence

As a youngster, I grew up in the city of *River Rouge, Michigan*, a suburb of Detroit. This was a city with two sides of the track. The east side was exclusively white and the west side was predominantly black, with a few white families living there. Housing on each side of the city was comparable. This was due in large measure to the fact that jobs were plentiful because *The Rouge*, as it was called, was in an industrialized area.

When the United States got involved in World War II, the factories in the area converted to war time production. People from various parts of the country, especially the South came to the area for work, and many home owners, including my family would take in persons who wanted to rent a room. Business was booming and the jobs were plentiful. However, this fact also raised concerns among the residents. River Rouge became a potential prime target for air raids. I would often accompany my Aunt *Mary Lou* during air raid drills at night as she would stop at the homes of some in our community instructing them to cut off their lights or face stiff penalties under the blackout regulations.

The Rouge River which flowed into the Detroit River brought traffic, industry and population growth. Railroads complemented the shipping facilities and factories making various automobile parts. A person could become a homeowner in a relatively short period of time due to the availability of jobs. *Great Lakes Engineering Works*, a Rouge industry was the builder of ships. Nearby, in the City of *Dearborn* was the *Ford Motor Company*. Although it is often called the *Ford Rouge Plant*, its name is derived from its location three miles upstream on the Rouge River. This plant, along with other automobile manufacturers made Detroit the *Motor Capital* of the world—often referred to as the *Motor City*.

My next door neighbors were white. They were polish and very friendly. I would often hear them having a good time playing polka's on an accordion. They would frequently extend an invitation to me to come and join them when they had a party, however, I never did. One of their relatives, who lived nearby played on my baseball team. He was a very good pitcher and the issue of race was never discussed.

The high school was midpoint between the two communities. White and black students would interact with each other at school and then return to our respective homes on different sides of the tracks. The overall racial composition during my time there was roughly fifty-five percent white, forty percent black and five percent Asian and Hispanic. There were several black owned businesses; however, all were located on the west side, including a black owned hospital; which was the only hospital in the city.

Race relations were generally amicable. However, there were occasional incidents where race could have been an issue. A black kid whose nickname was *Smoky* decided to attack a white kid at school for no apparent reason other than the kid was at the wrong place at the wrong time. *Robert,* who lived in my neighborhood, was black. He observed this and asked Smoky why he attacked the kid. Smokey's response was because he wanted to. Robert asked how Smoky would like it if someone did that to him. Smoky, who was a gang leader, said no one would do it.

I'd found out through the school grapevine sometime later that Robert decided to show Smoky the error of his miscalculated brashness. He'd shown him what it was like to be attacked for no reason. During the assault, Smokey's head was struck on a banister requiring the attention of a nurse.

When I arrived home, I observed approximately 12-15 guys walking by my house with Smoky. I went out and asked where they were going and I was told by *Bert,* who was the biggest and toughest in the group that they were going to Robert's house to get him for what he had done to Smoky. I went back inside and ran out the back door and down the alley to alert Robert. When I arrived at his house his mother informed me that he had just left to get the bus and go to work.

Upon leaving his house I observed Robert a short distance away waiting on the bus. I ran to alert him about the gang coming to get him so that he could run before they got to him. I also told him that I would help him fight but there were simply too many of them for us to fight. He didn't appear too concerned.

He said, "I'll be okay."

At that point the gang saw him and began coming to get him. To my astonishment, Robert told me to get back. He was well dressed in shirt and tie with a nice hat.

As the gang approached, Bert served as their point man. Bert approached Robert, with Smoky lurking in the midst of the gang with a huge bandage on his head. Bert yelled at Robert and said,

"Why did you beat Smoky up?"

Robert, with his right hand in his pocket responded, "What do you plan to do about it?" At that point Bert threw a right fist at Robert. Robert avoided the blow and then pulled a switchblade out of his pocket and to everyone's surprise began cutting Bert.

The gang rushed toward Robert, and then Robert pulled a gun out of his left pocket to shoot whoever approached. Like the Biblical Red Sea, the gang parted and either hid behind trees or cars leaving Bert and

Smoky, who was too weak to run begging for their lives. Bert was on his knees along with Smoky pleading for Robert not to shoot them. I looked at the expression on Robert's face. He had the demeanor of a person who was trying to decide whether to let them live or die. The gun had been put to Bert's head and a caution was made to Smoky that if he moved Robert would kill him.

The mother of another boyhood friend *George* had come out on the porch. She knew Robert well. She began yelling and pleading with him.

"Robert, Robert—don't kill the boy—don't kill the boy!"

She got Robert's attention. He seemed to slowly come out of a trance. As he looked at Bert he noticed that Bert had a gun in his waistline. He retrieved the gun and asked what he had planned to do with it. He took the gun and beat Bert in the head with it. Bert leaned forward on his hands and knees crying like a baby. Robert kicked him in his rear and then went over and beat Smoky again. Then he told both of them if they ever threatened him again, he would kill them. Both Smoky and Bert were bawling like babies. Then he told them to run like the cowards they were. They did. He took the gun Bert had and threw it in the sewer. He brushed himself off; waited for the bus and went to work. No one bothered him again.

This was one of the very few encounters that involved students of different races and in this case, a black student had come to the aid of a white student who was being beaten by a bully.

The only other incident of a racial nature involved me. The white drum major in the high school band called my white girl friend, who was also in the band, a *Nigger-Lover*. When she informed me of this, I sought him out and proceeded to punch him out until he apologized. One of the things that made this community a racially cohesive one was the success of the basketball teams. It was a source of community pride and racial harmony. We won more *Class B* State Championships than any other school in Michigan.

Whites and blacks would go on both the east and west side for sporting events, especially baseball, and the major shopping area in the city was located on the east side without anyone experiencing any acts of racial hostility.

My immediate *family* was comprised of my grandfather, grandmother, four aunts, and two uncles, two other uncles by marriage and an older female cousin and an older male cousin. I lived in a house where my grandmother and oldest Aunt *Fannie Mae* lived on the same floor, and where another Aunt *Georgia* and her husband *Jake* and their daughter *Fannie Lou* lived upstairs with her husband, *Henry*. My two uncles made what could at best be described as cameo appearances at our house—neither had any substantial involvement in my life.

Sometimes I Feel Like a Fatherless Child

One aunt *Katherine McCroskey* lived in a house next door with her husband *Alex* and another aunt, my favorite aunt *Mary McGhee* lived a block away with her son *Dan Jr.*. Her husband, Dan, a World War I veteran had died from the lingering effects of the war. Her son, Dan Jr., was eight years older than me.

Fannie Lou, who was 10 years older than me assumed the role of an older sister and Dan Jr., assumed the role of an older brother. Fannie Lou, along with Dan Jr., taught me how to drive and Dan Jr., taught me how to box and how to be good playing the game of baseball. He would take me to games in which he participated. He had the most substantial male influence in my life and I, unwittingly inculcated many of his values and lifestyle. He would marry three times and I would do likewise.

Even though Dan and I had a close relationship, there were strains in our relationship. Occasionally, it became evident that he resented me being in the household and competing for his mother's attention. This situation would become exacerbated when his mother would compare us and more often than not have more complimentary things to say about me.

There was one occasion where Dan got into a physical altercation with his wife. I grabbed him from behind and held his arms to prevent him from hitting her again. He had one-half of one of his fingers missing due to an injury. While holding him and mistakenly assuming that his wife would flee, she took her teeth and began viciously biting the remaining finger stump. He hollered loudly and I was uncertain what I should do while still holding him. Finally, his wife ran out of the house and I released him. Dan angrily looked at me and told me with a threatening demeanor that if I ever interfered with him again when he and his wife were arguing, he would kill me. Since he was a policeman, with easy access to guns which he kept in his dresser, I took his threat seriously. Fortunately, no similar incident happened and he and this wife soon divorced.

My Aunts Mary Lou and Kate had periodically impressed upon me that when I became an adult, I should make something out of myself. By that they meant I should not spend my life working in a factory. They wanted me to become a teacher, doctor or lawyer. They would often say in your job you should not have to pick up anything heavier than a pencil. Two of my aunts, Kate and Georgia would work in the homes of whites washing and ironing their clothes and cleaning their houses. My aunt Mary Lou would do the laundry and ironing at her home for a white family. Throughout my childhood, nothing was more strongly impressed upon me than the fact that I had to do something positive with my life.

My first experience with racism occurred when I was approximately 10 years old and went shopping in nearby *Dearborn*, Michigan with my aunt Mary Lou. It was a hot summer day and we stopped at an outdoor soda stand for refreshments. My aunt ordered two drinks for us, and as I eagerly reached for mine, my aunt slapped my hand and said,

"Wait."

She asked the man serving us to serve us in glasses as others were using rather than the paper cups we had been given.

He looked at her and said, *"We don't serve Niggers in glasses."*

My aunt responded angrily saying, "Well you keep your drinks!", as we angrily walked away.

When I became a high school senior, one of my girl-friends was white. She called me at home one day and my aunt answered the phone and could tell by her voice and diction that she was white. When she handed me the phone, she looked at me with a concerned expression on her face.

"That sounds like Mr. Charlie's daughter on the phone." She said.

I smiled, took the phone and talked for a while.

When the conversation ended my aunt said, "You better be careful Junior messing around with Mr. Charlie's daughter. You don't know what those people will do to you for messing with their daughters."

I smiled but never had any intention on ending the relationship.

As the years went by, my aunt Mary Lou expressed disappointment in her son Dan. She said I had none of the advantages he had as a child. His father had left him a nice sum of money and he had squandered it. And she said he got a job chasing black folks and locking them up as a policeman while I seemed to be doing more with my life. Understandably, this did not set well with Dan and some resentment began to emerge.

Nonetheless, my cousin Dan Jr. encouraged me in my sports activities. He gave me my first boxing lessons and on occasion would work as a corner man when I participated in the local boxing tournament. He seemed to take pride in my achievements. He also taught me Judo. We would spend leisure hours tossing baseballs and snagging fly balls at one of the local baseball fields.

Fannie Lou was very special to me. She taught me how to dance and would always see to it that I had Halloween costumes and birthday parties. We would decorate Christmas trees together. She and her mother also made a special effort to be certain that *Santa Claus* would always leave me nice gifts; I woke the entire house up one Christmas morning when I saw a brand new *Monark* Bicycle under my Christmas tree.

Fannie Lou also introduced me to the entertainment world of downtown Detroit. I vividly recall my first trip to Detroit's famed *Paradise* theatre. She took me to see *Cab Calloway* and his band. I recall Cab, in a white suit dancing, sliding, and tossing his head in a manner so that his hair would get the women excited as he sung his inimical *Hi-de-ho*. As I grew older, I would get my first driving lessons from her, and eventually easy access to her automobile.

When she eventually moved out of the family home into her own apartment, I had access to it where I could spend "quality" time with female friends.

When she died years later, unexpectedly from head injuries allegedly sustained in a fall, I was married and living in California. As I approached the entrance to the funeral home to view her body, my first glimpse of her casket as I prepared to enter the door caused me to lose my composure. I collapsed at the door, and broke into tears. Her death was too difficult for me to accept. Home would never be the same without her. I would spend much of my time during this trip reflecting on our relationship and how much she meant to me. I looked at places that were seemingly insignificant to others where she and I had done something together. Slowly I came to accept the fact that she was no longer a telephone call away. All that would be left for me were the memories that would last a lifetime.

I learned years later through a mutual friend who was a close acquaintance of Henry, Jr.—Fannie Lou's son—that Henry Jr. believed that his mother's second husband, Charles had thrown her down the steps in their home in a fit of anger that eventually resulted in her death. Her first husband, Henry, Sr., had died in an automobile accident. The relationship between her second husband and Henry, Jr., had never been a good one. After brooding about this for a number of years, Henry, Jr., who was married and living in Cleveland decided to return to the

Rouge and badly beat Charles. His actions resulted in Charles being hospitalized.

My aunts' always saw to it that I had nice clothes and spending money. When Easter arrived, I would always get a new suit and shoes. My Aunt Fannie Mae provided me my first insight into what life was like in the South. When I learned that she was contemplating visiting relatives in *Alabama*, I blurted out that I wanted to go. Her demeanor changed immediately.

With a somber expression on her face, she said, "Junior, we would never take you to the South. You have too much mouth; you would get all of us lynched."

I didn't know how to react, so I quietly walked away wondering whether she was really being truthful and what in my behavior would prompt that kind of response. I remembered that comment years later when a young *Emmit Till* was killed in *Mississippi* for whistling at a white woman. I thought about this when I was in the navy and en route to *Norfolk, Virginia* to get a plane to Europe.

My grandmother, Lillie Bell Palmer, nurtured me with love and food. I never went to bed hungry. She was born in 1866 in *Crenshaw County*, Alabama. Born one year after the end of the Civil War and raised in the South. She would be a living witness to a history of race relations that she would occasionally share with me. Her father, Caesar Fonville had been a slave in and around Hickory and Pine Grove, Alabama. His wife, Ransey Fonville had been a Native American; a member of the Cherokee tribe.

She would tell me stories about *Old Man Curl Fonville*, the white slave owner who bought my great-great grandfather, and how *good* he treated his slaves. By this she meant that he did not whip them. By contrast my grandfather's relatives were treated badly by their slave owners. My great-grandfather, *Ake* Palmer was a runaway slave who changed his name to Palmer to avoid capture and the brutality that would beset him if captured. He was the son of *Wash Morrell* and *Mathie*, who had been slaves in *Hickory Grove*, Alabama. Ake would live in a place near Hickory Grove which ironically had the name –*Sellers Station*.

Ake married "Lou", and she would give birth to Noah Palmer, who eventually married *Lillie Bell* Fonville, and she gave birth to nine children, one of whom would be my mother, Mollie.

My grandmother was the person who disciplined me when I misbehaved; which was frequent. The concept of "time-out" was foreign to her experience. It was either a "switch" or an ironing-cord to my back or bottom. Eventually I learned that if I jumped under a bed when she was swinging at me, it was difficult for her to reach me. When she came to one side, I would scoot to the other side until she got exhausted. She was not abusive, but a stern disciplinarian whom I loved.

Whippings usually came from skipping school or stealing something like peaches and pears that I'd eat or tomatoes from gardens that I used to throw at automobiles with my friends.

The family chores for me varied. Essentially they consisted of assisting my grandmother around the house. During the spring, Summer and Fall, this may have consisted of sweeping inside and outside the house, washing dishes, running errands and occasionally helping with the washing of clothes. I always enjoyed going to our local grocery store that carried customer's charge accounts. The grocer knew everyone, and invariably, I charged some sweet delight as a treat. When the cold months arrived, I had the responsibility of chopping wood and hauling coal from the coal yard so that it could go in our pot-bellied stove in the living room. This along with sufficient blankets and quilts was our primary source of heat.

Frequently, my friends and I would, contrary to warnings from our families, sneak over to the railroad tracks and obtain coal that had fallen off the railroad cars. Generally, no questions were asked about our resourcefulness. However, on one occasion, a cousin who lived in the adjacent community of *Delray* was playing on the railroad tracks and his foot got stuck between the tracks and a log under them. He was decapitated by a train. This incident more so than any parental warnings had the greatest effect on me as well as others—it caused us to cease going to the railroad tracks for coal.

The days of the week that I least looked forward to were weekends—this would mean the weekly bath in a circular aluminum tub placed near the stove so that I could keep warm. My cousin Fannie Lou generally assisted me with this task. When I got older my grandmother, convinced that I could wash myself clean, delegated this responsibility to me.

On those occasions when I was out-of-money, and my Aunt Fannie Mae's purse was not handy, I would get a popsicle stick, chew gum, melt it with a match and go to a newspaper stand and put the stick with gum on the end into the change portion of the newspaper stand to retrieve enough money for myself and friends to go to a movie and treat ourselves. Those were fond times that reminded me of just how crafty we were.

The truant officer was a frequent visitor at my home. I took pride in being one of the best thieves in the neighborhood. The items that I stole were usually petty items from the dime store or making a raid on someone's apple, peach or pear tree. However, if I knew friends who needed a baseball glove or other equipment, I was resourceful enough to go to one of the stores in our community and get it for them. Eventually, I was given the name *handyman*.One incident that caused a problem for me was when I observed a large silver object shaped like a globe sitting on a pedestal in a neighbor's backyard. I wondered if it was solid. I threw a rock at it and it shattered. I fled the scene. Unfortunately, someone had seen me. The penalty was a thrashing with an iron-cord.

The main influences in my life were females and my cousin, Dan Jr. The influence of my uncles for the most part was minimal.Except for occasional money to see a movie and purchase treats, there was no substantive involvement with me. My uncle Alex would occasionally try to get me to assist him in yard work, and I would, but I also made every effort to avoid it.

Although each uncle generally treated me well when they were around; they were not around that often. My uncle *Dorsey* worked and spent most of his leisure time away from home with various women. He envisioned himself as somewhat of a *playboy*. Periodically, he would let me ride around with him in his bright, shiny car that he always kept polished. He was the first of my uncles to die.

Uncle *Sezar* had three distinct characteristics: (1) He was a superb auto mechanic even though he had no formal education. His services were always in demand. His attitude seemed to be that if a car had a motor, he could repair it. He was never unemployed; (2) His *Achilles heel* was that he liked to drink and would frequently get intoxicated. When this occurred he would invariably come home where he would sleep until he was sober and then go about his regular routine; (3) He had an inimical laugh, often after he drank a fifth of liquor. The laugh sounded like the Russian word, *"N-yet"*.

My friends and I enjoyed trying to imitate him. He would demonstrate a good sense of humor and laugh at our poor imitation. He wanted to teach me how to work on cars, but I had no interest whatsoever. I did not like the idea of getting my hands greasy and dirty.

There was one occasion while intoxicated and angry at what he perceived to be the special treatment my grandmother afforded me, he hurt me. He called me a *bastard.* I knew that this meant a child born out-of-wedlock. It hurt, but there was nothing I could do about it except go to my room and try to forget it but I never did. With rare exceptions the memories of my childhood were quite good.

I watched the fathers of friends interact with them. I quietly yearned for such a relationship, but it was non-existent. That was a void in my life but I tried not to dwell on it since there was nothing I could do about it.

My Uncle Alex would take me to baseball games to see the Detroit *Tigers.* This was our team until the Cleveland Indians signed *Larry Doby,* the first black baseball player in the American league, and subsequently, the legendary *Leroy "Satchel" Paige* in 1948 when they were in a pennant race.

I recall vividly the first time *Cleveland* came to town with these players. This was a memorable experience. We were there. We sat in the bleachers and they were packed with black folks. When the starting pitcher for the Cleveland Indians got into trouble and put men on base, the pitching coach came to the mound, signaled the bullpen and the crowd became silent with anxious anticipation. Finally, he emerged, Satchel Paige. There was a thunderous applause from the crowd, especially the black folks as he walked slowly to the mound. Black Tiger fans found themselves rooting unabashedly for the *Brother* who had become a living legend in the Negro League. His first pitch was his legendary *hesitation* pitch. Strike one!

And the crowd roared again. After a few more pitches Satchel retired the side without a run scoring—another thunderous applause. It felt odd to root for a team other than the hometown team. Yet, it was easy to have a sense of pride in what was being accomplished by one of *us*.

When he retired, one sports writer, *Gordon Edes* of Yahoo Speaks wrote, *"He won more games than Cy Young; he struck out more batters than Nolan Ryan; he pitched in twice as many games as anyone else and had a persona than rivaled Babe Ruth."* He was the first black pitcher on an American league All-Star team. *Joe DiMaggio* called him the best and fastest pitcher he ever faced. He was elected to the Baseball Hall of Fame in 1971. The first Negro Leaguer to be so honored.

Jake, my Uncle who was married to my Aunt Georgia and lived upstairs over me worked at the Ford Motor Company. He rarely missed work and he enjoyed drinking *Stroh's* beer, smoking *Camel* cigarettes, hunting, eating chitterlings, pigs-feet and playing cards on the weekend. He would occasionally slip me something to drink and take delight in watching my reaction to strong liquor which I found distasteful.

On one occasion after a fresh snowfall, I was hunting for pheasant or rabbit tracks in an area near my home. I had my slingshot and was eager for a kill. Eventually, I flushed out a rabbit and chased him for a couple of miles. The rabbit decided to seek refuge among wooden logs used as a foundation for railroad tracks. I could not flush him out so I ran home to get Jake's assistance. He laughed and said the rabbit was probably miles away by now. Nonetheless, he came with me to be of whatever assistance he could.

To our surprise, the rabbit was still snugly secluded in the logs. Jake, without any hesitation, moved a log and quickly reached in and grabbed the rabbit by its ears, yank it out, and without missing a beat, broke the rabbit's neck with a *karate* chop. I was impressed.

I viewed Jake as a combatant. Although I was barely seven years old when the 1942 race riots broke out in Detroit, I remember Jake and his brother along with my Uncle Sezar and other friends eagerly loading the trunk of Jake's car with guns and ammunition to go and participate in the race-riot. I wanted to go along and join in the fight, but they would not allow it.

Unfortunately, Jake's consumption of alcohol occasionally caused problems. He could talk and curse non-stop for hours. I liked the way he cursed and would try to imitate him. When I did I was chastised by an aunt or my grandmother.

While intoxicated, Jake and my aunt Georgia got into an argument on the front porch. Jake pulled out a switchblade with the intent to stab her. Fortunately, the police had been called and the only thing that prevented him from stabbing her was a bullet in his leg shot by a Detective. The next morning, I made a special effort to dig the bullet out of the wall as a souvenir. My aunt forgave him. When he got out of the hospital, he went back to his regular routine—Work, drinking, smoking and eating his chitterlings and weekend card parties and playing the numbers. Fortunately, he never threatened my aunt's life again.

Playing the numbers was a daily ritual among many of my family members. My aunt Kate built her house on the money she received when she hit *313*. One night I had a dream and looked it up in a dream book and played *265* and when that number came out I received around fifty dollars. As the years passed, I was amused to see the States take over the numbers business by calling it *The Lottery*.

There was another memorable occasion that involved Jake. While acting under the influence of alcohol, he cursed at my Aunt Kate. When her husband Alex came home from work and discovered this, he immediately came next door and went upstairs to beat Jake. When Jake saw him coming he ran into his bedroom, crawled out the window, jumped off the roof and fled. He did not return until he knew that Uncle Alex had cooled off. He never cursed at Aunt Kate again.

No one in my immediate household had graduated from high school. My grandmother had difficulty reading and my cousin Fannie Lou had dropped out in the 11th grade. Dan Jr., who lived a block away had graduated from high school, but he was not really involved with me on a day-to-day basis. Thus, no one monitored my academic progress in school. Hence I approached education with a Laissez-faire attitude.

Sometimes I Feel Like a Fatherless Child

When I flunked the sixth grade, other than my personal embarrassment, there were no repercussions. My primary interests were music and athletics. I excelled in them. Years later—while in high school—I earned my varsity letters in baseball and swimming. I was a diver on the swimming team and I won the championship in my weight division in boxing in my senior year fighting a guy from a neighboring community. I earned honors in regional and state music competition.

Academically, in other subjects, I considered a grade of "C" a good grade and a grade of "D" meant that I passed but did not do too well. I did not realize the full significance or implications of this until it was too late.

There was one unforgettable moment that occurred one evening as I came home to get something prior to going to band rehearsal. When I went into my bedroom and turned on the light, a rat, the size of a small cat jumped off my dresser and fled out-of-sight. I hunted for it with a broom to no avail. Eventually I gave up the search and left the house. I assumed that it had found a crawl space somewhere in the wall and sought refuge there. By the time I returned from band rehearsal, I had forgotten about the rat.

This was in late fall and it was cold. When I went to bed I pulled a quilt up over me to keep warm and went to sleep. Later, in the wee hours of the morning, I awoke due to warm breathing on my neck near the jugular vein. It occurred to me that it was the rat. I quickly reached up and grabbed him by his tail and slung him as hard as I could into the wall. He screeched loudly and disappeared. I searched but could not find him. A couple of days later we could smell him. Apparently his neck was broken when thrown into the wall and he crawled away and died.

When I reached the age of 15, my grandmother had to go to the hospital for an operation on her foot. She had been diagnosed as having *gangrene* as a result of an ingrown toe nail and her foot was going to have to be amputated. She sent me 50 cents by my aunt Kate, with the message that she missed me. I was not allowed to visit her. I was told that she would be home within a few days. A day or so later, I observed my Uncle Alex arriving home with Aunt Kate in the car crying. I was puzzled why she was crying. Uncle Alex got out of the car with a somber expression on his face. He helped Aunt Kate out of the car and I ran over to her.

"How is Mama?" I asked.

Looking at me with tears streaming down her face she said, "Baby Junior, Mama is dead!"

I was devastated! I could not believe my ears and I couldn't speak. I ran away and went under the porch of my house and began crying like a newborn baby. They pleaded for me to come out, but I could not do it for a long time. It never occurred to me that the only mother that I had known was going to die. I suddenly felt very alone. What was I going to do?

Ironically, Fannie Lou's husband Henry had been killed in an automobile accident a day or so afterwards when a drunk driver hit him head-on as he and friends returned from a night out on the town. We had a double funeral, with both bodies kept in our living room prior to being taken to the church for their final rites.

ADOLESCENCE

During most of my adolescent years, my recreation consisted primarily of either playing baseball or managing a baseball team during the summer and going fishing in *Grosse Ile*, Michigan. Boxing and other activities such as swimming, or summer jobs shining shoes or selling watermelons off *Louie Dumbroski's* truck also occupied my time. To qualify to sell Watermelon's, Louie would ask, "Can you holler?"

"Watermelons..!   Get your nice, ripe watermelons!" I demonstrated.

After passing the test, my salary was $3.00 and all the watermelon I could eat for a day's work.

As I got older I acquired other jobs delivering newspapers, mowing lawns and shining shoes at my own shoe stand at a nearby grocery store. During the winter, I shoveled snow and spent my leisure time playing ice hockey, sledding and hunting.

Life with Aunt Kate and Uncle Alex

When my Aunt Kate told me that she and Uncle Alex wanted me to move in with them after my grandmother's death, I did that. It was not long before I realized that my life had changed dramatically. My Aunt wanted to select my friends, and she had a fetish for cleanliness. She would use roman cleanser in her dish water and insisted that I put toilet paper on the toilet seat when I had to use the bathroom. My uncle insisted that I help him with lawn work and my aunt insisted that I help with the dishes. Although it was occasionally irritating, I had no problem performing these tasks. However, the time came when I felt I had to leave.

One afternoon I put a warm bottle of soda pop in the freezer portion of the refrigerator. I forgot it and it burst. My aunt went into a tirade and let me know that perhaps she had made a mistake asking me to come and live with her. I let her know that I did not ask to come and live with them — she had asked me.

On another occasion, while cleaning a pot that had been used to cook with, I accidentally put a dent in it. Again, my aunt became angry and I let her know once again that I did not ask her to take me in — she asked me. My Uncle felt I was being disrespectful to her and slapped me. That was it. He was too big for me to fight so that night I packed a few things and left without their knowledge.

I went a block away to a friend's house. I tapped on his basement window and he let me in and that is where I spent the night trying to decide where I would go next. It was summer and the next day I went to the elementary school outdoor basketball court to play basketball. While playing in a game my cousin Dan, who, by this time had become a police officer came by in his patrol car and signaled for me to come over a fence and get in the car. He told me that I had upset Aunt Kate and she had filed a report with the police that I was missing. My attitude was one of indifference and anger. Dan did not want to listen or understand my point of view. When he told me that he would have to take me to the police station that did not bother me, I had been there before.

The Reform School Stint

Upon arriving at the police station I was greeted by Sergeant *Pittman*, a friendly white policeman who I liked. We had previous contact with each other. Basically, he told me that I had upset my aunt and she was coming to get me so that I could go home with her. I told him in a somewhat brusque manner, that I wasn't going home with her.

"You have a choice. You can either go home with her or you can go to Reform School." Sergeant Pittman said in a stern voice.

I quickly responded that I will go to Reform School. When Aunt Kate arrived to get me, she was distraught and in tears. Sergeant Pittman informed her of my decision, and to my delight, she cried even more and left.

Shortly thereafter Sergeant Pittman took me to the Reform School in Detroit. I was processed in and soon saw some of the fellows from my neighborhood.

One in particular was a guy whose nickname was *Teeny*. He was a notorious thief—if it wasn't tied down he would steal it. He put the rest of us to shame. He had no respect for anyone's property. He was looked upon with little or no regard or respect by my buddies.

After 24 hours in Reform School, Sergeant Pittman came to see me. He told me that my aunt, *Mrs. McGhee*, said that I could come and live with her. I was pleased to hear this. I left with her and remained there until years later when I joined the navy.

I experienced none of the problems with my Aunt Mary Lou that I had with Aunt Kate. My relationship with Aunt Kate thereafter was cordial and respectful. She was always helpful, but I rarely visited her and would never live in her house again. Dan had married and he and his wife were also living with his mother. Most of the people in my community either owned their homes or lived with relatives until they could buy one. This was not difficult because jobs were plentiful.

I had often listened to Elder Morton on the radio sing *"Oh When the Saints, Go Marching In"*. This was Sunday afternoons at 3:00 p.m., when I lived with my grandmother. Occasionally, I went to *Union Second Baptist Church* where I eventually got baptized. However, when I moved in with my Aunt Mary Lou, things changed. I was in church every Sunday. She was an Usher. And one of my most enjoyable moments would occur when the minister would get on a roll, and my aunt would start clapping her hands, shaking her head, jump up and start shouting. People around her would say: "The Spirit has hit her" and begin fanning her when she, along with other females fainted under the influence of *the spirit*.

Some things were slow to change. One day, Detective *Manning* came to the house to see me. My aunt was not home, neither was Dan. He said the owner of the local hardware store had filed a complaint about thefts at his store. Detective Manning, through good detective work identified the three best thieves in the community. I was one of them. My immediate response to the suggestion that I was guilty of any crime was to deny it. And as I peered from my doorway at the police car, I saw the two other thieves in the back seat laughing at me. We knew each other well and they knew I was lying. They had squealed on me. Detective Manning promised amnesty and no criminal record if everything was returned. It took three or four trips to the attic, but I returned everything I had in my possession and was not arrested. I could not return such items as balls, bats, and gloves that I had supplied for one of the baseball teams I either played on or managed. That experience brought an end to my days as a thief.

God's Grace

There were times when, but for the Grace of God, I could have killed someone or been killed. *Louis McCants*, a big tackle on the football team decided as a prank to show off for his friends. He grabbed all 130 pounds of me in the locker room in the high school gym and dumped me in a locker to the glee of his friends. When I got out there was laughter on everyone's face but mine. One of the observers, a classmate, whose nickname was *Spike,* knew me well. He knew that I would not take such an insult without retaliating. Since Louis was too big for me to fight, I knew how to get him.

When school ended, I rushed home and got a cinder block and my Ryder B.B. gun while Louis went to football practice. I went to the overhead of a viaduct that the kids on my side of the track had to come under when they returned home. I secluded myself and waited for the football players to return from practice. As Louis, Spike, and a few others began to emerge from the cover of the viaduct, Spike grabbed Louis' arm and advised him to look up before he continued. Fortunately, he did. When I saw him I tried to drop a cinder block on his head. It hit the ground, barely missing him. He immediately charged up some steps to get me. I stood my ground and began shooting him repeatedly with my B.B. gun. He turned and fled. I had honed my skill with the B.B. gun by shooting rats in the alley behind my house that crawled out of their holes in the evening to eat garbage from holes in the garbage cans. I got Louis good with shots to his head and back as he turned and fled. He didn't bother me again.

Noel Myricks

A High School Encounter

While attending my high school band rehearsal one evening, there was a light snowfall. I thought it would be fun to tease one of the young girls in the band by throwing soft snowflakes in her face. She was, *Dorothy*, the little sister of Spike, who had the reputation of being the toughest guy in my class. Fortunately, he and I were friends. His sister told me that she was going to get me. I laughed because I did not take her threat seriously. I assumed that what she meant was that when the opportunity became available, she would either hit me with a snowball or slap me.

After a subsequent evening band rehearsal, Dorothy hid and rushed at me to hit me with some snow. I pivoted and she missed, slipped and fell. I laughed at her making her more furious. Again, I did not take her threats seriously because I regarded all of this as lighthearted humor—a prank. That point of view almost cost my life.

A week or so went by and I forgot about the incident. On a subsequent evening after another band rehearsal, I was standing outside the high school chatting with some friends, and suddenly I felt a sharp pain right below my lower right rib cage. It felt as if someone had punched me as hard as they could. I grabbed my back and looked around. There was Dorothy, with a scowl on her face, walking away looking at me with a menacing expression.

"Wow! That little girl can hit" I said to one of my friends, *Jerry*, as I held my back. Another friend, George said:

"Man, you are bleeding badly." Another friend, *George* said in observation.

When I removed my hand, it was covered with blood. I was shocked. I asked Jerry to look at my back.

"Man, blood is running from your back like water from a faucet. That girl stabbed you. You better get home and get to a doctor" he said.

I was astonished. I got home and was rushed to the hospital.

After examining me the doctor said, "If you had been stabbed two inches higher, your lung would have collapsed and you would be dead." And then he said, "What are you people out there in River Rouge doing to each other? We had someone here last week whose skull was fractured after someone had beaten him in the head with a blackjack."

He was talking about my neighbor across the street, *R.T.* He got into a fight with *Gus* and was getting the best of Gus, when a friend of Gus', who had moved to the Rouge from Detroit, handed him a rubber bicycle grip filled with lead to make a blackjack. Gus began beating R.T with it until he collapsed.

When I returned home to recuperate, Spike came to see me after his sister had been arrested.

"Man, what did you do to my sister?" Those were actually the first words out of his mouth. I was shocked.

I said, "Excuse me. What did I do to her? I believe I am the one who almost lost his life because she stabbed me in retaliation for me throwing a handful of soft snow in her face and teasing her. You should know that I would not have done anything harmful to her. You would have beaten me from one end of the block to the other end."

Nothing much was said after that and he left without further delay. Our relationship was never quite the same after that. There was a trial and her attorney tried to raise as a defense that I slipped backwards and injured myself. That defense did not prevail and she was found guilty and sentenced.

By the time I got to the 11th grade, I was more active in sports and band and things were going rather smoothly. Yet, on one summer evening, I saw a fellow who I knew from another neighborhood. He was bringing one of the girls from my block home. I was confident that they had been fornicating. I had no interest in the girl, but I was restless and decided to pick a fight and beat him for recreation.

The following day I learned that he was a member of a gang and they said they were going to get me. That didn't bother me. Shortly thereafter, some of my friends went to the pool room in their neighborhood, and I saw *Lamar*, one of their gang members.

"Lamar, I understand that you and your boys are going to get me. I'll be here for a while, why don't you go and get them." I said.

He put his pool stick down and left in a hurry. No one returned after about an hour, so my friends and I left. As we returned to our neighborhood, there was a voice behind us, yelling under the street lights.

"Noel, Noel, here we are, come on back."

It was *Shuge*, who I knew well. He had played on one of my baseball teams. I did not know that he was one of the gang. It was late and all of us had curfews. I turned to Jerry, Charles and George and said,

"What do you guys want to do? Should we go back and punch these guys out, or ignore them and go home?"

Jerry and George said they were indifferent. *Charles*, who was the best boxer in the group, began pounding his right fist into an open left hand.

"Let's go hit a few people up side their heads and then call it a night." He said.

We were confident that we could beat them so I agreed. When we got within striking distance, we suddenly found ourselves confronted with guns, knives and a Boy Scout hatchet. We had not anticipated this. With rare exceptions, when fellows in the neighborhood had a dispute, it was resolved with fists, not weapons. Everyone froze. The leader and mouthpiece for the gang whose nickname was *Pickle* sized up the situation.

He said, "We only want Noel and his boy, George." No one moved for fear of losing their life. George and I were slapped and punched while guns, knives and hatchets were kept at the ready in the event we fought back.

My Revenge

Finally, they let us go and told us to run before they started firing. Everyone ran but me. I was humiliated and wanted revenge. The fight had not been a fair one. Upon arriving home, I went into my Cousin Dan's bedroom, got his *'38 Smith and Wesson* out of his drawer, and checked it to be certain it was loaded, put it in my belt and headed out of the house. My Aunt, who was in bed, asked me where I was going at that time of night. I told her that I had to run an errand and would be back shortly. My intent was to go to Pickle's house, ring the doorbell and if he answered, shoot him in the face at point blank range. If a parent answered the door, I had planned to ask to speak to him, and when he appeared, shoot him in their presence. All I could think of was how I had been humiliated in an unfair manner, and desperately I wanted retribution.

Sometimes I Feel Like a Fatherless Child

As I walked across the front porch and proceeded down the steps, my cousin Dan arrived home. He had parked his car in front of the house rather than in the garage, and was proceeding up the steps as I was descending. He asked where I was going that time of night, and I told him that I had to run an errand and would be back shortly. He looked at me immediately noticing how disheveled I was.

"What is wrong with your face?" he asked.

I tried to turn my head away so that he would not look too closely.

"What is that in your waist?"

Before I could answer, he grabbed my arm and thrust his hand in my waist and pulled out his gun. He forced me to return inside and tell him what had happened. And then he asked that I let him handle it as a police matter.

Several years went by before Pickle and I talked again. He and my Cousin Dan had become *Shriners*. Dan had died and Pickle and I found ourselves standing shoulder to shoulder at the cemetery where a few final words were being spoken. I had become an Attorney and Pickle had gone on to get married and have a family. I looked at Pickle for a brief while.

I said to him, "The man whose body is lying there in that coffin had a profound effect on both of our lives. If it had not been for him, you would be dead, and my life would have gone in an entirely different direction than it has."

Pickle smiled and said, "I know. He told me"

The Challenges Ahead

The remaining time that I spent in high school was devoted to trying to earn the high school band award which was given, if deserved, to the best graduating high school band musician. When my name was called at graduation to go on stage and receive it that became my finest experience in high school. I had earned something I worked very hard to achieve.

Due to sheer ignorance, it never occurred to me that a certain grade point average was required for admission to major colleges and universities. I simply thought that the only requirement was high school graduation. One of my best friends, who was class Salutatorian, had been admitted to the University of Michigan. He had an older sister and mother who closely monitored his work. We never discussed academics and no one ever monitored my academic endeavors. My interests were elsewhere.

When I applied for admission to Michigan so we could be together, assuming I would be a good addition to the band there, I experienced a rude awakening. I also thought it would be wise to apply to Michigan State University where another classmate had been admitted just in case I did not get into Michigan.

Needless to say, I was disappointed when I received letters of rejection from both institutions. So, I decided I would attend Wayne State University. I submitted an application and went there for an audition to try to get a music scholarship. I became excited after my audition when the person conducting it informed me that I would receive a scholarship once I had been admitted. That puzzled me. He explained that after the Admissions office admitted me to the university it was at that point that I would get the benefit of a scholarship. I became nervous. Another obstacle suddenly appeared. Predictably, my application for admission was denied. The laissez-faire approach to my high school education was having dire consequences for me.

Eventually, I was admitted to Highland Park Community College, but my ego would not allow me to go there, especially with friends going to more prestigious universities.

I had graduated from high school on a Friday and began working full-time at the Ford Motor Company in the foundry on Monday. The pay was good but I could not envision myself spending the rest of my adult life there. I did not like the hot working conditions and I would come home dirty and sweaty. I simply felt that I could do better than this with my life. I didn't want just a job and a paycheck. I wanted to do something I thoroughly enjoyed that would give me the satisfaction of being personally fulfilled. I decided that I would join the Navy and become a Navy Musician and eventually become a music teacher.

Noel Myricks

NAVAL EXPERIENCES AND TRAVELS

I went to the Navy Recruiting Office and told the recruiter that I wanted to be a Navy Musician. He asked about my music background and requested documentation of it. I provided this and he told me to come back in a week. When I returned I was informed that I did not qualify to be a Navy Musician but that I could still join the Navy. I was stunned. I had been supremely confident that I would be accepted into the Navy music program. I had to choose between keeping my job at the Ford Motor Company, which was unthinkable or joining the Navy—I joined the Navy

When I informed my Aunt of my decision, she inquired why I had not joined the Army as her son Dan had done. I told her the Army was not for me. I could not envision myself sleeping outside in all sorts of weather and being shot at or having hand grenades thrown at me. I recalled seeing a scene from the Korean War on television. I saw a snow-covered mountain and then heard a bugle. The snow on the mountain began to move and as I looked intently at that scene, I saw American soldier's emerging from their sleeping bags that had been covered by snow during the night. That was not a life I had envisioned for myself. The day I departed, I got up without waking my aunt and left. When I got to the recruitment facility, I telephoned my aunt to tell her I had gone, I loved her and I would be mailing my clothes home when I got to boot camp. She was disappointed that I had not awakened her. I told her that I wanted her to rest.

Upon arriving in boot camp at *Great Lakes, Illinois,* my company Commander asked whether any of us could play musical instruments. I raised my hand and was told that I would be in the boot camp band. I thought this would be a pleasant experience but little did I know how it would affect my future in the Navy.

The boot camp band practiced at a facility that housed a unit of the U.S. Navy bands. I watched them rehearse and yearned to become one of them. After a rehearsal I asked their Conductor how I could become a Navy Musician. He told me that I should have applied when I joined the Navy and I would have been sent there for an audition. I told him I did apply and was told that I was not qualified. A puzzled look came across his face. He said the recruiter in Detroit could not determine my qualifications; they had to send me there for an audition. When I asked why the recruiter would lie, he stated that if I came into the Navy as a musician, the Naval School of Music would get credit for the recruitment, and not the recruiting officer in Detroit who is under pressure to meet a monthly recruiting quota.

I asked whether I could still get an audition and he replied in the affirmative. I told him that my main instrument was French horn, which I played in concert band and bass drum which I played in the marching band. This was October and I had not touched a horn since June.

I asked if I could have about a half hour to warm up and get familiar with the horn and he agreed.

He had me play a few scales, the Second Trumpet part to the Washington Post march (which I had played countless times), and then some solo horn parts from three major concerto's that I had performed in high school. My high school band director had made me memorize the solo parts of most of these songs. When I finished, he looked at me and said when you complete boot camp you'll be going to Washington, D.C., to attend the Naval School of Music and upon your successful completion there you will spend your remaining tour of duty as a navy musician. I was elated, but the elation was short-lived.

Ensign Smith

Upon returning to my barracks, I was not allowed to have sufficient time to make up my bunk bed before inspection by Ensign Smith. When he inspected and inquired as to whose bunk it was, he ordered me to come to his office after inspection. I mistakenly assumed that he would verbally harass me and perhaps have me perform some calisthenics. I was partially correct. One of the black seaman recruits pulled me aside to try and prepare me for what to expect. When he told me that he was crying when he left Ensign Smith's office I was surprised. I said to myself, this kid is from the South; I'm from Motown, this

Officer is not going to make me cry regardless of the harassment.

When I went to Ensign Smith's office, he was sitting there with a white Chief Petty Officer whose insignia on his sleeve indicated that he had been in the navy for at least 20 years. The harassment began. I had to come in and out of his door on several occasions; stand at attention while being verbally assaulted. And then to my astonishment, I was slapped hard across the face and punched several times in my body while being ordered to stand at attention. And then it got worse. I could take the punches—I had been hit harder by guys I had boxed in high school who knew where to punch and how to execute their punches for maximum effect. But I had not been prepared for what happened next.

And then Ensign Smith said, "I don't know how a black b. . . . Like your mother could give birth to a nigger like you."

At that point, tears began to roll down my cheeks. It took every measure of self-control I could muster not to punch out both the "Officer" and the Chief Petty Officer with him. I knew I could easily knock both of them out. I had been an amateur boxer since the 5th grade and became a champion in my division in my last year of high school. It was humiliating and difficult for me not to retaliate.

I also knew that if I lost my composure, I would win the battle but lose the war. I would get a dishonorable discharge and in all likelihood spend time in a Federal

Prison. I also did not want to be a source of embarrassment to my family. I had been in fights most of my life. They would not say anything, but I felt they would wonder why I could not take what these Officers were dishing out.

I asked myself, *-Who would a trial judge believe – a "nigger" from the Detroit area or an "Officer and a Gentleman" and a Chief Petty Officer who had served his country "honorably" for more than 20 years?*

The final insult was a kick in the rear as I was dismissed from the office. I vowed that before I died, I would locate Ensign Smith and kill him. I learned through my research on the Internet 50 years later, that he was alive and where he was living in Maryland. I found myself conflicted between a strong desire for revenge and my spiritual beliefs that such revenge belongs to Jehovah and not me. Romans 12:19 had its impact on me.

It states, *"Vengeance is mine. I will repay says Jehovah."*

My religious beliefs prevailed. Further research revealed that Ensign Smith had been dishonorably discharged and punished later for killing a sailor under his command.

Angered by that experience in boot camp, I vowed when I left that if another white person crossed my path who insulted me in any way, shape or form, they would never forget me. Shortly before I left boot camp while doing mess hall duty, one of my white peers got in a dispute with me and he suggested that we go outside to settle it. The fight lasted less than 30 seconds when he screamed: "I quit; I quit" after I broke his nose with a hard right cross after faking a left jab to his mid-section causing him to lower his arms to defend himself. Others would follow for most of my time in the Navy.

NAVAL SCHOOL AND EXPERIENCES ON THE SEA

I got out of boot camp in December 1955 and returned home for a brief vacation before going to the Naval School of Music in Washington, D.C. When I left my hometown, I knew that I would be embarking on an uncertain journey. I did not know where it would lead or what I could expect, yet, I was confident that I was prepared to accept whatever challenges I would encounter.

Shortly after I arrived home, I was surrounded by some of my closest boyhood friends. The air was filled with the Christmas spirit. The bitter experience of boot camp slowly faded away. I spent most of my time with *Andrea*, who became a Jet magazine pin-up girl while I was in boot camp.

I met her while driving on the east side of Detroit one afternoon. She was a stunning powder-brown girl who I saw walking into her house. I immediately parked the car and waited for her to appear again. When she did not come outside, I went to the door and was greeted by her mother. I felt that I had two options:

(1)   To drive off and forget her.

(2)   To go to her house and try to get to meet her.

I introduced myself to her mother and told her that I saw this beautiful girl come in, and when she did not come out again, I assumed that this was where she lived and I wanted to meet her. I told her mother I had dropped some friends off and decided to drive around the area because I wanted to see the *Brewster Center*, where *Joe Louis* had honed his boxing skills and that was when I saw her.

Predictably, her mother was taken aback. She smiled in disbelief. She politely asked whether I was some sort of *nut*. I laughed and convinced her that I had control of all my faculties. I was well-dressed and driving my cousin Dan's new '55 Oldsmobile. She smiled, apparently impressed with my audacity and appearance and invited me to come into the house for further questioning.

Upon entering her home, I nodded to a fellow who I subsequently learned was her son. Without being asked to do so, I began to pull various documents out of my wallet to verify my identity, and suggested that she could call my cousin Dan, at the police station in River Rouge where he worked as a policeman. I quickly took the initiative to do that and had her talk to Dan to confirm my sanity.

She called her daughter out of the bedroom. When I saw her, I said, "Yeah, she's the one—she is definitely the one." Her mother told her that I wanted to meet her.

Needless to say, Andrea was surprised at my aggressiveness and approach. She greeted me with a beautiful smile. We spent the next hour or so talking.

Apparently, I made a positive impression. We dated on several occasions shortly before I went into the service.

We resumed where we left off when I got home from boot camp. We would probably have gotten married if I had remained in Michigan. But, to paraphrase *Tennyson*:

". . . there is so many miles and so far to go and such little time and so much to do."

After two weeks, I left for Washington, D.C., and the Naval School of Music. I arrived with excitement and enthusiasm in January 1956. As I approached the school, I heard *Rimsky-Korsoff's "Flight of the Bumblebee"* being played with what seemed like dazzling speed and precision by a young trumpet player.

The adrenalin began to increase, and I could barely control my excitement. If I had not been carrying my duffle bag, I would have run to the School. Upon entering the School and signing the roster, I immediately inquired how many French horn players were there and who the best was. I was eager to meet that person and let him know that I would be looking forward to challenging him for his reputation.

Someone said, "I believe there are about 14 and *Pete Mackey* is the best; he is up in the auditorium practicing now."

Before I could be assigned a bunk and locker, I deposited my bags at the roster desk and hurried to the auditorium to size up my competition. As I entered the auditorium, Pete gave me a casual glance and a pleasant nod to acknowledge my presence as he continued to practice.

Within a short period of time, I found myself in what might be described as a semi-state of shock. I had heard good French horn players in State competition, but this guy was phenomenal. I could not believe what he was doing with his horn. When he paused to take a break, I asked him about certain notes that I heard him play. He confirmed my worst suspicion. He had been playing and playing comfortably an entire scale above the generally recognized range of the instrument. I had never seen or heard anyone do this before.

He had played these notes with relative ease and the speed with which he played was more reminiscent of a trumpet player rather than a French horn player. This was my introduction to the U.S. Naval School of Music.

As the months passed and I became familiar with the other Horn players, I was pleased to learn that Pete Mackey was in a class by himself. During my time there, there were approximately 14-16 horn players, and in my opinion there were only two who were better than me. One had been the solo horn player at the University of Arkansas before he decided to join the Navy. The other was Pete Mackey.

While there I recorded Mozart's First Horn Concerto with full orchestral accompaniment and graduated with an average which certified me as a solo horn player. One fellow, who was a graduate of the *Eastman School of Music* told me that he could get me a scholarship to Eastman when my tour of duty was over.

My time at the music school was one of the most enjoyable periods of my life. I had the opportunity to spend countless hours with my horn, and be stimulated by the environment and competition at the school.

However, there were times when I experienced a sense of anomie at the School. After our rehearsals, several of the students would participate in *jam* sessions. All I could do was observe and listen. I was a classical musician. I envied those who could "jam". They could play the music of my people. I could only play *Mozart, Bach, Beethoven, Tchaikovsky* and other classical writers. This sense of alienation plagued me throughout my naval experience and eventually persuaded me not to pursue a career in music.

One particular incident really had an impact. While sitting around watching some of the guys play jazz, a lean, handsome young black male walked into the auditorium. He had recently arrived at the school and we had never met. He pulled his saxophone out of the case and immediately joined in. As the tempo picked up, he placed his instrument in its case and walked over to the piano and began to play it with considerable facility. Others who were standing around began nodding their heads in approval and snapping their fingers. Eventually, he got up played clarinet and then went to the percussion session and played various percussion instruments, and the room became crowded and excitement was in the air. When the session ended, I went over to introduce myself. I learned that he was *Steve Griffin*, out of the highly acclaimed *Cass Technical High School* in Detroit. That school had produced such great musicians as *Donald Byrd, Ron Carter, Geri Allen, Regina Carter, Lydia Cleaver*, vocalist *Diana Ross, Paul Chambers* and many others.

Steve would go on to have a career as a navy musician and became one of the founders of the navy's first jazz band, the *Commodores*. We would see each other again years later when his band was playing a concert in *Columbia*, Maryland. He told me that blacks could now get into the national concert band. And he had been one of the founders of the national jazz band.

When I was at the music school, blacks, regardless of talent, could not get into the National U.S. Navy concert band, which was based in Washington, D.C. We could go to the fleet bands and bands located at various duty stations in the U.S., and around the world but not the national band. One black fellow who had been the solo trumpet player in the concert band at the University of Illinois came out for an audition. He was very impressive and was offered an appointment in the band at the Naval Academy in *Annapolis*, Maryland. He declined the offer. He told the Commander of the school, thanks but no thanks; that if he could not get in the national band, then he would not join the navy and he returned to Illinois. This policy did not change until after the election of President *John F. Kennedy*.

Noel Myricks

Although the atmosphere at the School of Music was conducive to promoting a person's professional development, I continued to have problems in my interpersonal life that inevitably lead to physical altercations.

Everything in my background had taught me that I would be viewed as less than a man if I was challenged and did not accept the challenge. It was better to fight and lose, than turn the other cheek.

My first altercation was with another black student from *Gary, Indiana*. I noticed that *Woody*, as he was nicknamed, enjoyed the role of bully with some of the other young brothers. He was a very provocative person, often grabbing others in headlocks and asserting his dominance over them. He was well-built and appeared quite strong. He reminded me of a brown middle-weight version of *Rocky Marciano*. It was my hope that he and I would never get into a fight with each other. Unfortunately, it was written in the stars.

It occurred at lunch in the base mess hall. I was with Woody and another fellow musician who we called *Dowe*. Woody, sitting directly across from me and next to Dowe pointed behind me and said, "Look!" I turned to see what he was pointing at and saw nothing. When I turned to commence eating I noticed that a small carton of milk was missing from my tray. I asked where it was and no one said anything. Dowe signaled with his eyes that Woody had it.

I asked Woody to give me my milk and he feigned ignorance and refused to do so. I became angry and told him to keep his *"[expletive] hands out of my tray or else."* Woody appeared shocked that someone would challenge him.

He said, "What!"

And then he put his hand directly over my mashed potatoes as if to dare me to do something and I took my fork and tried to stab him in his hand.

He quickly jerked it away, but I did get a piece of his skin. At that point Woody appeared to go berserk. He jumped up from the table and wanted to fight right there. I refused to do so. He began to shove me all the way back to the music school and insisted that I was going to fight him or else.

I told him that I did not want to fight because I did not want to get a bad conduct discharge and get kicked out of the school, but that I would agree to meet him in the gym that evening and we could have it out. He enthusiastically agreed to this arrangement. He looked at me with a clenched right fist.

"I am going to break your neck." He said.

He said it with such conviction that I had cause for concern. I knew that if we got into a wrestling match I would have virtually no chance whatsoever because I was 6'0, slim at about 140 pounds and not a very good wrestler. Woody was approximately 5'11 and seemed to be a rock-solid 160-165 pounds and very strong. Yet, I knew I had to engage him in combat.

I got to the gym before him and began putting on boxing shoes that had been provided by the gym director. Woody entered shortly thereafter with a small entourage.

Upon entering he yelled out, "Where is he? Where is he?"

That startled me. The gym director saw that we had come there to fight and he quickly intervened.

He said, "You guys put on the gloves and go at it until one of you quit."

I breathed a sigh of relief. I was not in great boxing shape because my life had been a sedentary one since I arrived at the music school, but at least I was fighting him on my terms. This was what I wanted. I believed my boxing skills could offset his advantage in strength. I had spent too many hours at the Motor City Arena in Detroit observing the professionals, and in front of the T.V., watching the Friday night fights and honing my boxing skills in our school boxing tournament to be fearful.

When Woody was told he had to box me he said: "Fine! I'm going to splatter that sucker's brains all over the ring." He continued to look at me in a menacing manner while slamming his right fist into an open left hand, as if to give me notice of what to expect.

The gloves were laced by the gym director. We were then told to go at it. Woody came out of his corner with a wry smile on his face. My game plan was simple, Move like *Sugar Ray Robinson*, my boxing idol. When Ray fought *Jake LaMotta*, my friends and I were glued to the television; Ray would be the matador and stick the bull. Now, I was determined to be the matador and stick the bull until he was knocked out or quit.

I began to undergo a psychological metamorphosis. I could hear the words of one of the great corner men from our high school boxing tournament, *Marvin T.I. Turner*. He was our version of Ali's *Budini Brown*.

I could hear him coaching me saying, "Stick-him; stick-him; stick-him and move. Keep that left in his eye."

I knew this is what he would say to me if he were here. I began to smell blood and got ready psychologically for combat.

Woody came out of his corner and threw the first punch—a light left jab that I easily avoided. He smiled confidently and then swung a right-cross. I pivoted on my left foot and watched it go by. I quickly observed that he was holding his right-hand low; at his waist-line. I also noticed that when he threw a left jab he would drop his right hand and make his chin vulnerable to a left hook. I was puzzled. I wondered if he could be this deficient in his boxing skills with all his mouth.

I jabbed and moved—jabbed and moved. To my pleasant surprise I could easily reach him with my jab. He did not seem to know how to defend against it. After a couple of jabs I feinted a left jab to his stomach and when he moved his right hand down to defend against it, I hit him with a hard left hook on the chin that sounded like a bass drum. He blinked, smiled and confidently said: "That didn't hurt." Suddenly, I felt a surge of confidence. He was making mistakes that none of the neighbor guys who participated in boxing would make.

At this point I moved in for the kill. I gave him a shoulder feint and he went for it and I unleashed another left hook and his knees buckled and eyes appeared somewhat glazed. I mistakenly paused to see if he would drop. But he quickly recovered.

He smiled and said, "Good punch."

No one whom I had ever hit like that had said that to me before. That gave me cause for concern.

My jabs became harder as they found their mark directly on his nose. His eyes became watery. The more punishment I inflicted the more he seemed to relish it. He seemed to thoroughly enjoy combat even though he was being beaten.

I decided to try and set him up for a good solid right-cross on the chin, followed by a left hook which I had hoped would take him out. While in the process of trying to do this, I got careless. I saw out-of-the corner of my eye a round-house right hand coming directly for my chin that I could not avoid. When it hit the target, I saw red, white and blue stars. The pain radiated from my chin all the way to my ankles. I wanted to scream with pain, but my pride would not permit me to do so. I quickly tied him up until my head could clear.

He did not seem to know how badly he had hurt me nor did he know how to finish me. Finally, the gym director yelled, "break—break!"

I released him. I began to have some idea how *Jersey Joe Walcott* must have felt when a crude Rocky Marciano hit him with a right hand flush on the chin and took his heavyweight championship.

I decided to "stick and move—stick and move". It worked. Woody could sense blood and he moved in for the kill. He threw another right hand, but it was blocked. He smiled! I gave him a look of scorn to let him know two could play this psychological game of war.

I countered with a left hook which again, hit him directly in his face. He seemed more annoyed and irritated than hurt. At that point I decided that if I lost, someone would have to carry me out. Both of us were tired but I would not quit.

I stopped dancing, planted my feet and went toe-to-toe with him. Every time he exposed his face, he had a jab or left-hook in it followed by a quick right. I bobbed and weaved to minimize the impact of his blows. I managed to either block or slip them and counterpunch. Suddenly, right after a sharp left jab hit him in the nose and brought water to his eyes, he uttered words that were music to my ears.

He said, "I quit!"

I breathed a tremendous sigh of relief.

Angrily, he said, "Okay, okay, you beat me; you beat me, now let's get these gloves off and wrestle"

My rejoinder was, "Hey, we've already fought and you got your butt beat. You don't want any more of me."

What he did not know was that I did not want any more of him. My pride had kept me from quitting. The gym director intervened and said the fight was over. We had fought by the rules and I had won and it should stop there or we would be subject to disciplinary action. Neither Woody nor I pressed the point and never fought again.

Shortly thereafter, Woody would receive his orders and he was sent to a unit band. I felt a sense of relief that he was no longer around. I mistakenly assumed that this would be my last contact with him. Approximately a year later while in the fleet I would learn that of all the ships and duty stations with bands, Woody had been assigned to come to the one I was on. Shortly after arriving, he began his bravado again but this time it was somewhat subdued. It wasn't long before we would become the best of friends.

When he decided that he wanted to box a Greek fighter when we got to *Athens*, I became his corner-man and taught him how to develop his greatest deficiency – a good left jab to go with his powerful right hand. Eventually, when the time came for me to return to the U.S., I offered him the apartment that I had in *Nice, France*, which he gladly accepted. Years later after he was discharged, he came to visit me at my home in Michigan, but my aunt informed him that I was living in California. He became a music teacher in California and the recipient of numerous accolades.

A subsequent altercation at the music school was one that I truly regretted. A white kid from West Virginia who I liked was manipulated by one of his jealous fellow tuba players to fight me. He and I had a good relationship and in fact, I had been giving him boxing lessons at the gym. One day out of the clear blue he came up to me and demanded that I fight him. I was shocked and puzzled. When I refused to do so he told me that I would either fight him or he would physically assault me. He refused to give me any explanation about his change in attitude toward me. He knew or should have known that I could beat him, yet, without fear or apprehension, he insisted and threatened to harm me if I didn't.

He seemed to assume that strength and a high level of motivation would compensate for his lack of boxing skills. It didn't. We went to the gym, at his insistence, put on the gloves and got in the ring. He charged across the ring at me with a full head of steam. I hit him one time with a hard left jab that caused his nose to bleed. He ran right into it. Fight over, with blood splattering everywhere.

I felt guilty about this for a long time because I did not want to fight him, but could not avoid it. I subsequently learned that one of his fellow tuba players from Chicago had played the role of the Shakespearean character *Yago*, and had lied to him manipulating him into getting angry at me for no valid reason other than to have the satisfaction of seeing him get punched out.

My third and final altercation at the School of Music resulted in a disciplinary action – a *Captain's Mass*. There had been a rash of thefts in the barracks where I lived. Rumors suggested that the thief was another French horn player but no one had come forth with any proof.

One afternoon as I prepared to go into the shower, *Harry**, the alleged thief was standing near my locker talking to one of his friends who went by the nickname of *Moose*. When I came out of the shower, Harry and Moose were gone and so was some money that I had in my locker. When I inquired about the whereabouts of Harry, I was told that he had gone to the base movie theatre. I got dressed and went to the movie theatre and had him paged.

When he came out and saw me waiting for him in the lobby, he appeared startled. I told him to return the money he had stolen from me or I would whip his butt on the spot. He began to turn red in the face. He stuttered and proceeded to take my money out of his pocket, admitting that he had stolen it and spent some of it to attend the movie. He said that he would return the balance within 24 hours. Hands shaking, he gave me my money. Due to his act of contrition, I told him that I would not report him to our superiors, but if he ever went near my locker again, his mother would not recognize him when I got through with him.

Approximately a week later, two of his white friends, Moose and *Larry** decided that they would retaliate against me. While walking behind me, one of them whistled at me as though I was a woman and called me *Miss Myricks*. This behavior persisted notwithstanding my warnings to them to cease and desist. Nonetheless, they persisted.

Finally, one Saturday afternoon while resting on my bunk and engaging in a friendly argument with another sailor about which college football team should be ranked first in the nation; Moose and Larry walked in and commenced their harassment.

Larry said, "What does *SHE* know about football Moose—what does *SHE* know?"

They began laughing at me. The fellow I had been talking to had a shocked expression on his face. Annoyed, I got off my bunk, put on my trousers and walked to where they were. By this time, Moose had got in his upper bunk and his buddy Larry was standing nearby talking to him. I told both of them that I was warning them for the last time to stop harassing me, that I had enough of it. As I began to walk away, they laughed and continued the harassment. That was the straw that broke the camel's back.

I returned and told Moose to get out of his bunk because I was going to kick his rear end. His partner, Larry laughed.

He said, "Look Moose, she's getting mad, she's getting mad."

I whirled and unleashed a hard right fist across the bridge of his pointed nose and broke it with one punch. He screamed in pain as blood splattered. He ran from the scene toward the office.

"He broke my nose; he broke my nose." He screamed.

Now, with my back to him, Moose leaped from his bunk onto my back. My knees buckled, but I maintained my balance and gave him a judo flip over my shoulder. As he crashed into the nearby lockers, he slowly rose to his feet with fear on his face.

I told him that I had given him fair warning, now he belonged to me. I began a flurry of punches, left jab, right-cross followed by a left hook and he went down. I told him to get up and fight like a man or I would kick him. Slowly, bleeding, he got to his feet and grabbed his glasses off the bunk. Hurriedly he put them on.

"You can't hit a person with glasses; you can't..." he cried.

Before he could complete his sentence, a left hook to his head sent his glasses flying and Moose was down again. I told him that it was too late for that now. He should have thought about that after I had repeatedly warned him to stop harassing me.

At that point, one of their friends had come to the area and when he saw what was happening, he turned and ran out of the area screaming, "He's killing Moose; he's killing Moose!" I commenced throwing lefts and rights to the body and head of Moose as he staggered pitifully with only a wall or bunk holding him up. Finally, a Chief Petty Officer hurried to the scene and ordered me to stop. I thought about what the two racists had done to me in boot camp and hesitated to show Moose any mercy. I assumed at this point that I would be disciplined and kicked out of music school, and was prepared to accept the consequences. But I was determined not to take any more insults or offenses off any white person regardless of the consequences.

Captain's Mass

Charges of assault were brought against me and the base Chaplain showed up at the Captain's Mass with Moose and Larry. The Chaplain talked about how outstanding these two sailors were and their roles as altar boys at Sunday Mass, and the damage that had been inflicted on them by me. Moose was described as having a concussion, a black eye and a fractured jaw. His partner Larry had a broken nose.

When the Captain asked why I had attacked them I provided him with background information about the thefts in our barracks, the confrontation with their friend and his admission of guilt, and their subsequent harassment of me in retaliation. I told the Captain that I repeatedly requested them to stop their harassment and they refused to do so, until finally I had enough.

The Captain then asked whether I had ever been a professional boxer. I responded in the negative with no further comments about my boxing background and training. I told the Captain the entire incident would not have happened if they had left me alone but they refused to heed my warning and persisted in the harassment.

To the consternation of the Chaplain, all of us received the same punishment—washing pots and pans in the Mess Galley for a couple of weeks and temporary suspension of our other duties. I breathed a tremendous sigh of relief and was quite pleased that I would be able to continue in the music program.

After that incident, no one bothered me anymore. The black sailor's in the music program were quite pleased and would say to me discreetly, "I'll bet they will think twice before any of them mess with a *'brother'* again."

Time quickly passed. With no further distractions, I focused on developing my music skills and where I would be sent when I completed my studies. When I had my exit examination, I chose to perform the *Romanza* and *Rondo* movements in Mozart's Third Horn Concerto. I received a high rating and was eager to marry *Melissa**, a beautiful Louisiana-Creole who I had met briefly in my hometown when she was visiting relatives. She was a student at Southern University in Baton Rouge. She had come to D.C., to be with me with an expectation of marriage which I had promised.

Since every French horn player who had graduated before I did was sent to concert bands in places like *Honolulu*, *Treasure Island* in *San Francisco*, and the State of Washington, where they performed weekly shows on T.V., I assumed, based on my rating that I would be going to one of three places—the Brooklyn Navy Yard in New York, or naval bases in either Philadelphia or San Diego. I eagerly looked forward to going to one of these places. Finally, my orders arrived.

One of the Petty Officers approached me and said, "Myricks, your orders have arrived. Go down to the personnel office."

I was excited and rushed to get them.

I entered the office with a broad smile on my face. The clerk who greeted me said: "Myricks, you will be going to Com. Sixth Fleet."

Com. Sixth Fleet

When I heard the word *fleet* I almost fainted. My knees weakened. I could not believe what I had heard.

I said, "What! What is Com. Sixth Fleet? It sounds like water; I know I am not going to sea; no French horn players have been sent to sea since I have been here. Where is this place?"

I knew my rating was high enough to get a choice assignment. I began to feel a sense of numbness and anger. I wanted to hit someone. I had not felt such anger in a long time. I wondered whether this assignment was in retaliation for the fights that I had while there.

A First-class Petty officer who had been sitting at a desk behind me got up and walked over to me. He had a smile on his face an extended his hand to congratulate me. Feebly and with no desire to be discourteous, I shook his hand.

He stated that he had recently returned from Com. Sixth Fleet to come to the School of Music and go through the course required to become a Chief Petty Officer. He added that when he completed the course and became Chief, he would be returning to assume charge of the Com. Sixth Fleet band. He seemed thrilled and excited for me; but I was still in a semi-dazed state.

I was trying to figure out what happened and how this would affect my plans to marry Melissa and my life.

I kept mumbling, "Solo horn players don't go to sea."

As I began to regain my composure and listen more attentively, I couldn't help asking myself:

"Where is this place – Com. Sixth Fleet? I never heard of it."

He patiently explained to me that I should regard it as an honor to be selected for that band. It was an Admiral's band, and I would be on the flagship of the Sixth Fleet whose homeport was the French Riviera. My jaw dropped—The French Riviera? Did I hear him right? He said the homeport was a tiny fishing village called *Villefranche-sur-mer*. It was tucked between the city of *Nice* and the principality of *Monaco* and *Monte Carlo* on the Riviera. My duties would consist largely of ceremonial activities, and I would be able, should I desire to do so, live in an apartment or villa with others in France, wear civilian clothes and I would have a lot of free time. He said virtually all of the musicians live ashore.

He added that I would be on the heavy cruiser, the *U.S.S. Salem* and would have the opportunity to visit countries like *Italy, Spain, Greece, Sicily, Portugal, Lebanon, Malta* and other places in the *Mediterranean* area. And if I wanted to take leave, I could go to places like Paris or any other place in Europe. My jaw dropped once again. I had studied French in high school but earned mediocre grades, but the idea of visiting France, especially the Riviera and Paris fascinated me.

I was told that I would have a lot of free time on my hands and when we were in our homeport, the band members would rotate among themselves and play colors in the morning every two or three days and would be free to leave afterwards. The dance band would play cocktail parties for the guests of the Admiral, such as *Princess Grace* of Monaco or the Shah of Iran. He added that he was eager to return as soon as he was promoted to Chief Petty officer.

Upon learning that I would be going overseas, I became reluctant to get married. I was simply a Seaman and did not have enough status to take Melissa with me. And she was simply too beautiful for me to marry her and be thousands of miles away for approximately two years. I could not cope with my feelings of insecurity and the thought of someone else making love to her in my absence. When I informed her of my assignment, I also told her that I would be unable to take her with me and why. I also stated that when I returned, if we still felt the same, we would get married. She seemed hurt, but did not say much.

I was given the opportunity to return to my hometown for two weeks prior to going to Europe, however, I declined. I was eager to get to France before Christmas. Shortly thereafter, I was flown to Norfolk, Virginia where I would get a plane to France and experience the aura of the French Riviera.

En route to Norfolk, I had the opportunity to reflect on my experiences to date and what might lie ahead. The letters of rejection that I had received from some universities were viewed as temporary setbacks and not permanent defeats. I was prepared to do whatever I had to do to remedy my academic deficiencies and attend college when my tour of duty was over. I was glad that I had the opportunity to work in the foundry at the Ford Motor Company. I knew that it was not a place where I'd want to spend most of my adult life. Thus, the issue was not whether I would go to college, but where. I wanted to become a high school band teacher who also taught physical education. These two activities had been the source of some of the happiest moments in my life.

I had never been as far south as Norfolk, Virginia. I wondered what it would be like. I knew that it had the major naval base on the east coast, but I did not know anything else about it.

My stay in Norfolk was brief. Shortly after arriving at the base there and checking in, I decided to go with another black sailor to town. We got on a bus and after paying the fare I proceeded to walk down the aisle to try and find a seat. The bus driver called me to give me a ticket but I did not hear him. A white sailor I had just passed who was standing in the aisle got my attention for him.

He said, "Hey You!"

"Yeah..?" I replied when he got my Attention.

He looked at me with a scowl on his face and said, "Yeah? You better say – yes sir."

I looked at him as if he was crazy. I immediately clenched my fists.

"I do not know who you think you are talking to, but I will punch your lights out here and now" I said.

He turned his back and walked away. I got my ticket and had no other problems. When I returned to the base I decided to stay on it until my departure, which was a few days later.

Departure from the U.S.

I departed Norfolk in December 1956. There was a brief stop in the Azores, one of two Atlantic Ocean archipelagoes located about 800 miles due west of Lisbon, Portugal. I discovered that the word Azores means *Hawks*. Apparently, Portuguese navigators in the early 15th century observed hawks in great numbers over these islands, and this fact greatly influenced the choice of a name for this archipelago. This archipelago is comprised of nine major islands and several islets covering approximately 890 miles.

After a brief delay, we proceeded to a city in the *Rabat* region of northwest French Morocco. It was a seaport town named *Port Lyautey* on the *Sebou* River. I learned that I might be here for two or three days until additional transportation was provided to France. That was fine with me. It was fascinating to be in Africa, even if it was North Africa.

I was eager to get into the city and see the *Casbah*. In films, it had always been depicted as a mysterious place, filled with intrigue. The women in films had been shown wearing veils over their faces and the men invariably engaged in some sort of clandestine activity. It was my intent to visit the next day. As I began making arrangements to go to the city, I learned that an American sailor, acting under the influence of alcohol, had snatched the veil off one of the women in the city. His body was subsequently found floating in the Sebou river, with his genitals sewn in his mouth. My interest in visiting the city quickly waned, and I remained on the base.

Two days later I was awaken in the wee hours of the morning and told that I should pack immediately because my plane would be leaving for France. Within a short period of time I was in the air looking down at a city I had never really visited. Perhaps another time.

Noel Myricks

Cote d'Azur

The next stop would be the airport in Nice, France. As the plane descended, the view of the Cote d'Azur was spectacular. My heart was beating with excitement. I had read so much about the Riviera in my French classes, and had followed the exploits here of the international playboys like *Purferio Rubirosa, Aga Khan* and *Aristotle Onassis* with envy.

Cecilia Cooper, a beautiful black American woman had been selected as the beauty queen of the *Cannes* Film Festival. Never in my wildest dreams did I assume for one brief moment that there would be a period in my life when I would actually visit, let alone live, however briefly on the French Riviera. As a child growing up in Michigan, I had only been to three places outside of the Detroit area:

(1) Akron, Ohio, to visit relatives.

(2) Ontario, Canada.

(3) El Paso, Texas, where my cousin Dan took me, his mother and girlfriend on a short trip to revisit where he had been stationed while in the Army.

Upon landing at the airport, a car with an officer, an Ensign escort was waiting for me. I was impressed. It was December 21, 1956, a day before my birthday. I would celebrate it in the south of France. There was a nice chill and excitement in the air. As we proceeded from Nice to the bay in *Villefranche* where the ship was moored, we rode along the Promenade des Anglais. It is a wide and magnificent promenade bordering on the blue Mediterranean Sea. It extended the entire length of the city.

I observed young couples kissing and hugging each other. They displayed a sort of uninhibited affection in public that I had never seen in my country. The officer and I exchanged few words. I was mesmerized by the beauty of the place and the behavior of those I observed.

Eventually, we ascended the cliffs that separated Nice from Villefranche. As I looked back at Nice, it appeared as though it was a city that belonged in a fairytale. When we began to descend to Villefranche, which was located about four miles east of the city of Nice and six miles southwest of Monaco, I saw my new home – the flagship of the Sixth Fleet, the U.S.S. Salem moored in one of the deepest harbors of any port in the Mediterranean Sea. It was decorated with an assortment of lights and pennants; it appeared almost like a huge Christmas ornament. It was beautiful.

We proceeded down winding roads and past picturesque, pastel-colored villas. They seemed omnipresent along the cliffs. Finally, we arrived at the dock. A few feet away was the renowned *Welcome* Hotel, which would have among its many visitors, *Elizabeth Taylor* and her husband, *Mike Todd. Brigitte Bardot, Rita Hayworth, Anthony Quinn, David Niven, Sean Connery, Harry Belafonte, Noel Coward, Rex Harris, Josephine Baker, Somerset Maugham, George Harrison* and countless others had eaten there. Nearby was the internationally known restaurant – *La Mere Germaine*.

The squeaky-clean boat of Vice Admiral *Randall Charles "Cat" Brown* came out to the dock to take us to the ship. Cat Brown was the Commander of the Sixth Fleet and I was one of his musicians. When I learned that his ship would be my next duty station, I did some research on him and learned that he had been born in *Tuscaloosa*, Alabama in 1899. He had graduated from the Naval Academy in 1921 and served in both World War I and World War II. He was married, with two children; one who had recently graduated from the Naval Academy.

What I found particularly impressive was that he was a combatant. He had been in the battle of *Leyte Gulf* and in the landings at Leyte, *Luzon* and *Iowa Jima*. He had commanded the aircraft carrier – the *Hornet* a few days before the surrender of the Japanese, and had earned the bronze star.

He was described by those who knew him as *"a fearless operator in battle; cold, calculating, and one who would close with the enemy—a brilliant strategist and a diplomat."* He had also served as a former Chief of Staff at the Naval War College. He seemed to be a man who could be respected. I hoped his southern background would not cause problems for me. It never did.

Upon arriving at the ship, I was escorted to the musicians' quarters and a hot meal was prepared for me. To my surprise, there was only one person there. He was a pleasant, albeit stoic young man from Pennsylvania who introduced himself to me as *Beaver*. When I inquired about the whereabouts of others, he informed me that everyone else was at their apartments or villas on shore. He told me that he decided to stay aboard because he wanted to save his money for college. He also said that he had a girlfriend at home and he wanted to be faithful to her. His attitude seemed strange to me.

Periodically, I have thought about him and our conversation. Initially, I found it difficult to comprehend how a single male could be on the French Riviera and not have the time of his life. His values were obviously quite different from mine. As the years have passed, I have acquired a much greater appreciation and understanding of his values and what his parents did for him in instilling those set of values. I also hypothesized that he probably became an outstanding husband and Father.

I went to the Welcome Hotel the following day to celebrate my birthday and explore different sites in the area. I had a wonderful spaghetti dinner, with a very good red wine and French bread served by a crackling fireplace. I was made to feel like a treasured guest in this captivating place located near the bay.

The following day I visited Nice. I got lost and discovered to my pleasant surprise that I could recall enough of the French language to ask directions and understand the responses. Upon returning to the ship, I made a special effort to meet some of the other *brothers* who worked on the ship. I wanted to locate the nightclubs and get their insight as to where to go in Nice. I was informed that there was a USO in Nice that was nice, and I could meet people there. When I went there during the afternoon, I bonded immediately with some brothers from Baltimore: *Jay*, who I would nickname *Monsieur Jay* and his cohort *Bobby*.   We became, for the lack of a better expression – *running buddies*.

Jay was a boatswain mate on the ship and Bobby was an accounting clerk. Jay came to my attention as I watched him perform the *cha-cha* and *mambo* with an attractive French girl. I admired anyone with talent, especially if they could perform well in the *Afro-Cuban* idiom. And Jay performed extremely well.

Bobby was also a very talented dancer and had exceptional interpersonal skills which he used to great advantage in attracting some lovely French women. The three of us became inseparable.

We attended a popular club later that evening – the *Whiskey ago-go* and after that a club which afforded me an opportunity to meet additional brothers and women. As I walked into the last club, the sound of Mambo music permeated the atmosphere. This was my first exposure to a discotheque environment. Most of the females appeared to be extraordinarily beautiful. One in particular got my attention. She was engrossed in a very sinuous dance with another brother from Baltimore whose nickname was *Spider*. She was a voluptuous blonde from Denmark whose name was *Anita*. They seemed to epitomize sensuality in action. Prior to this time I had never seen a black man with a white woman this beautiful in my entire life. I, along with others had engaged in interracial dating with white girls in high school, but the women, especially the *Scandinavian* ones in this club were quite different from the ones back home. It was a memorable evening.

Eventually, I met all 24 members of the band. In addition to myself, there were three other black band members. One was *Vancy Bulluck.* He was from *Rocky Mount*, North Carolina. He became my closest friend in the band. I gave him the nickname *Bull.* He was a second-class Petty Officer who always had my back. He played clarinet and saxophone. He and another brother *Roscoe,* a drummer from Boston were close and had an apartment in Nice. The third brother was known as *Chip.* He was a drummer from New York who would frequently play at jazz sessions whenever the opportunity permitted itself in any port.

The band members would play colors in the morning on a rotating basis. The bulk of my leisure time was spent in Nice, Villefranche, Monte Carlo or Cannes. I was offered the opportunity to share an apartment with three band members who were white. We got along great and would frequently have dinner together at the restaurant owned by our landlord. It was located on the first floor of our apartment complex. However, when the evening arrived and it was time to party, more often than not, I was with the brothers from Baltimore, New Jersey or New York.

One of them taught me to cha-cha, mambo and *meringue,* and I took full advantage of this new skill. Invariably, I could almost always be found in one of the three clubs in Nice:

(1) The Whiskey Club.

(2) The Whiskey Ago-go.

(3) A jazz club popular among college students and occasionally European tourists.

In addition to cultivating a taste for French coffee, *gelati* and other deserts at the different cafes, I would often visit the *Place Massena,* which is the main square in Nice. Artists would frequently put their paintings on display there. It was a short distance from the Promenade des Anglais. Another short distance away was shops with various items on display. All of this was a short walking distance from where I lived.

Cruising Europe's Bluest Sea

After the holidays, the ship went to sea. I looked forward to this because I needed the rest. It had been an exciting time for me. I looked forward to visiting other places and learning new things.

I had been on pleasure cruises between Canada and Detroit while in high school, but land had always been in sight. This would be a different experience. As we cruised out of the harbor of Villefranche I would find myself experiencing that which I had heretofore only seen in movies or on television. There would be no land in sight; just water, the sky and other ships. In some instances, the other ships were not readily visible except through radar contacts.

One of the duties the musicians had while at sea, in addition to playing music, was to work in what was called *Flag plot*. This was the Admiral's tactical and navigational control room. It was adjacent to the Admiral's cabin and had radar and sonar units. We, along with the quartermasters and other specialists monitored submarine, ship and air traffic. On occasion when there was concern about something, the Admiral would be alerted and he would come out of his cabin, view the problem and recommend a certain course of action. Occasionally, General Quarters would be sounded, which meant prepare for battle – just in case. At that point the entire ship would become combat-ready in the event the cold war became a hot one.

When a guided missile cruiser, the *U.S.S. Canberra*, notified the Admiral that a Russian *MIG* was flying too close for comfort, apparently monitoring our exercises, the Admiral allegedly instructed its Captain to *bring it down*. There was silence in Flag plot. Apparently, as the officers on the Canberra began to proceed to follow these alleged orders, the MIG turned and flew out of the area and a conflict was avoided.

Noel Myricks

There were inquiries about the incident and considerable media attention, but denials were forthcoming. Some Congressmen had expressed concern that such behavior by the Admiral could be construed as an act of war. This did not appear to have an adverse effect on the Admiral's career.

When these military exercises were concluded, we sailed through the *Straits of Gibraltar* into the Atlantic Ocean en route to *Lisbon*, Portugal. Upon arriving in Lisbon, Jay and I went to purchase some custom-made camel hair top coats. We had spent some of our leisure time at sea designing them. We wanted to be better dressed when we returned to France.

We also engaged in sightseeing while in Portugal. This included visits to the *Tower of Belem*, the *Moorish Alfama Quarter* and to the *Manueline Jeronimos Monastery*. We saw Lisbon's monument to the Navigator, *Prince Henry*, which was built in honor of the ruler who sponsored many of the seafaring explorers, including *Magellan*.

I was surprised at the complexion of the Portuguese people. In my ignorance, I had mistakenly assumed the people would have tan complexions like Mexicans. These people, for the most part, appeared no different than the average white person, with a slight tan, which suggested the Moorish influence. After several days in Lisbon, we returned to the Mediterranean Sea.

Sometimes I Feel Like a Fatherless Child

I enjoyed the rhythmic motion of the ship at sea. Eventually, I acquired *sea legs*; which was learning how to maintain one's balance while walking as the ship moved through the water. There was something akin to a quiet serene beauty in observing other ships, like the battleship *Iowa* cruise through the water off into the sunset. This had somewhat of a mystical attraction and an appeal that duty on land could never provide. The cool sea breeze seemed to cleanse the nostrils and reinvigorate tired bodies.

It was intriguing to watch the rhythmic motion and chants of the boatswain mates when they worked as small groups chanting in a melodious fashion or calling cadence while scrubbing the ships wooden deck. They would use poles similar to mop handles inserted into small bricks. They would sway and call cadence together. When moored in a harbor, the boatswain mates would chip the barnacles off the ship and paint it again to maintain its spotless appearance. This was a constant reminder that I was on the Flagship of the Sixth Fleet and its impeccable appearance had to be maintained.

There were no *slobs* on the ship and none would be tolerated. Personal appearance and the appearance of the ship were of the utmost importance, especially since there were frequent visits by guests. Gunner's mates would clean and polish the ship's big guns. On rare occasions when I went to the quarters of the Marines that were on board, some would always be observed spit-shining their shoes or pressing their uniforms so that they could maintain their impeccable appearance.

Noel Myricks

After remaining at sea for a short while, we cruised to the great Rock of Gibraltar. My time there was spent viewing the sights of *St. Michael's Cave*, a place where there were *Barbary* apes that had been described as the last wild apes of Europe. There was a network of tunnels used by *General Eisenhower* and the allied command during World War II. An aura of secrecy still surrounded these tunnels, with frequent hints that the current technology contained in them would be of considerable value in keeping the Straits of Gibraltar open long enough to enable the Sixth Fleet to get out of the Mediterranean sea and into the Atlantic Ocean where our chances for survival would be greater in the event of hostilities.

Although the Mediterranean Sea was a beautiful body of water, it was no place to fight a sea battle. The water was described as so clear that airplanes could easily detect submerged submarines and destroying ships would be tantamount to shooting fish in a barrel. This was not comforting news to a person serving on a prime target – the Flagship of the fleet.

One person on the ship who perked my curiosity was a civilian. He invariably was almost always at the Admiral's elbow, especially when it appeared that there might be trouble. I discreetly inquired about him with one of the quartermaster's in Flag plot. I was told that he was a Ph.D., from *M.I.T.*, who served as an advisor to the Admiral about the use of atomic weapons. I made no further inquiries.

Sometimes I Feel Like a Fatherless Child

When we arrived in Gibraltar, Jay and I spent our time purchasing *Harris-Tweed* sports coats and English sport caps to wear when we returned to France. After a few days in Gibraltar, we returned to sea.

While at sea, with the expectation of remaining in the western Mediterranean, I learned that we would proceed to the eastern Mediterranean. Problems arose in *Hungary, Greece* and *Turkey* which involved the *Island of Cyprus.* En route we stopped at the *Island of Malta* for repairs. This small country lies south of Sicily and is about twice the size of Washington, D.C. Its key industries consisted of ship repair and shipbuilding.

The Malta dry-docks were the country's largest employer. Although Maltese and English were the official languages of the country, Italian was commonly spoken. This tiny country had been ruled by the *Phoenicians,* the *Romans,* the *Arabs,* the *Normans,* the *Knights of Malta* and the French. It became a British crown colony in 1814. *Valetta,* the capitol of Malta had two of the best natural harbors in Europe.

Malta was strategically within easy striking distance of Greece, Turkey and *Egypt.* During the Second World War, Malta had suffered severe aerial bombardment from the German and Italian Air Force. Even though I visited some of its famed tourist sites, what I would remember most about Malta were three things:

(1) The pungent odor of its limburger cheese which seemed to permeate the air.

(2) Observing men who worked on our ship removing food from our garbage cans to take home to their families.

(3) that it was the first nation in the world to prove that people of different nationalities, specifically, eight different countries could live together in relative peace and harmony.

When we left Malta and cruised east, the overall mood of the crew moved from one of acceptance of a situation over which we had no control to one of making the best out of the experience. En route, we encountered for the first time, high winds and rough weather. I had my first experience with sea sickness. Upon going to the dining area to eat, food trays had to be held with one hand while sailors tried to eat with the other. The smell of food became nauseating.

It was not uncommon to see sailors jump up and rush to the toilet to vomit. Older sailors with more time at sea seemed the least disturbed. They would often smile with delight at those of us who were younger trying to cope with the turbulence. On one occasion when I decided to go topside, hoping the fresh air would bring some relief, I looked at other ships and to my astonishment, some, especially the smaller destroyers seemed to get completely covered by the sea. They seemed to be like corks that would be under water and then pop up again.

Upon observing the waves becoming higher than some of the ships, I decided that it was time to go below deck, get in my bunk and rest as best as I could. Trash cans would slide around our compartment until someone would take the initiative and secure them. Eventually, I heard for the first time an expression on the loudspeaker that would become common place:

"Secure all hatches—secure all hatches."

One did not need an I.Q., over 50 to understand that this meant things would get rougher at sea and the ship would have to become watertight.

A peaceful calm returned to the sea the following day. I went topside to see what, if any damage had occurred. To my amazement several of the vehicles that we had aboard which served as transportation for the Admiral and his staff were badly damaged by the waves. Some appeared as though they had been in a demolition derby even though they had been secured by several chains.

Some sailors on the destroyers had lost their lives. They had been washed overboard and ships were patrolling for survivors. None were found; only the remnants of their empty life jackets. When the search was concluded, we moved from the Mediterranean to the *Aegean Sea* and cruised to the port of *Piraeus*, Greece.

This was a welcome sight for all of us. There were rumors that *Archbishop Makarios*, the patriarch of the Orthodox Church in Cyprus and the leader of the movement to unite Cyprus with Greece would be free soon. He had been exiled to the *Seychelles Island* by British authorities. When he was first exiled in 1956, the Greek government had reacted angrily to British policy on Cyprus and the exiling of the Archbishop.

This uncertainty as well as uneasiness in Lebanon caused to a large extent by the agitation of Egypt's Nasser conflicted with U.S. interests and prompted our presence there.

Athens, Greece

When tensions began to cease, we arrived at *Piraeus,* Greece. Friends and I got a taxi to Athens. It was good to feel land under our feet again. We went to a Greek Tavern in *Plaka,* the oldest neighborhood in Athens and had an enjoyable meal. We indulged in *bouzouki, ouzo* and wine as well as other Greek dishes and enjoyed ourselves for the remainder of the evening.

The following day there was a *Happy Hour* at the USO. It had an amateur music contest. I, along with some of the brothers from New York and New Jersey decided to sing some Rhythm and Blues songs. We were not the *Dominoes, Drifters,* nor *Jackie Wilson* or *Clyde Mcphatter,* but the audience acted as though we were because we put on quite a show. I may not have been able to play jazz, but I could sing Rhythm and Blues, and as a result female companionship was very positive and forthcoming.

The remainder of my time in Athens was spent exploring such Athenian sights as the marble *Acropolis* and *Parthenon*, the *Temple of Wingless Victory* and the *Erectheum*, with its porch of maidens; the Greek *Theater of Dionysus* and the Roman *Theater of Herodus Atticus*, and the *Mars Hill*, which is best known as the place where the Apostle Paul preached. I went to the colonnaded promenade where, *Socrates*, one of the greatest of Greek Philosophers taught.

In the years ahead, when I would study the thoughts of Socrates in his pupil's book, <u>The Republic of Plato</u>, as well as those of Plato and *Aristotle* and enjoy arguing about Greek philosophies in the coffee shops around college and university campuses in the San Francisco bay area, or at the tables outside the book stores in the North Beach section of San Francisco while sipping Café espresso, I would reflect on these experiences and my formal education would become even more meaningful.

Friends and I went to an opera in a lovely amphitheater and subsequently savored the white wine and exquisite food of Greece. In addition to visiting the monuments of antiquity, I had the opportunity to view the Presidential Palace with its evzone guards who wore their traditional white kilts in colors of red with black caps and red clogs and their ceremonial changing of the guard. They also guarded the *Tomb of the Unknown Soldier* as well as the Presidential mansion and the gates of the Presidential Guard Training camp.

I found the visit to Greece extremely enjoyable. There was one particular incident that had quite an impact on me. Jay and I, along with our dates were standing at the end of a very long line waiting to get into a movie theatre. The theatre manager approached and asked us to follow him. He escorted us ahead of the line and into the theatre to choice seats and declined to accept our offer of payment.

This sort of treatment was unimaginable in my own country. It was difficult for me to conceive of a white American male being this gracious and considerate to black men with white female companions in the United States. Indeed, I thought about the pictures that I had seen of crowds of white Americans with their children gathered around the lynching of black men, cheering and smiling as they were being castrated, and their genitals and other body parts being kept as souvenirs.

Patmos, Greece

The visit to Athens did not seem to last long enough. We returned to sea for almost two weeks to maintain a state of combat readiness and then proceeded to the tiny Greek island of Patmos. This would be the first of several trips there. We performed at a wedding for some politically influential person. The ceremony was quaint. The bride and groom followed the band with a host of others in what can only be described as a ceremonial march. Everyone seemed elated at the festivities and the Admiral appeared pleased with our performance.

Patmos is a tiny Greek island where John the Apostle wrote the book of *Revelation*; the last book in the Greek Scriptures. This was around 95 A.D. It is a place with pine covered hills and caves and a 10th century *Monastery of John* as well as the grotto where he received the Revelation. It has often been described as the *Jerusalem of the Aegean*. After a few days there, we cruised to the Greek Island of *Rhodes*.

Rhodes, Greece

When we came into *Mandraki* harbor we saw the statutes of two iron deer which are at the site of the *Colossus* – one of the seven wonders of the ancient world. Several sailors quickly got into swimming suits and headed for the beach shortly after we docked. Others went shopping, looking for souvenirs that would cost considerably more if purchased in the United States.

Rhodes had been built by the *Knights of St. John*. It is mountainous, with scented forests of pine and fir. It is a place of such scenic beauty that *Julius Caesar* had chosen to study there. It had its bazaars, mosques and attractive houses. The Crusader battlements of the Knights of St. John and the Palace of the Grand Masters were sights to behold as we walked on some of its narrow cobbled streets.

When tensions appeared to have eased, we were elated to learn that we would be returning to the western Mediterranean and our home away from home –

Villefranche- sur- mer. En route there, we would briefly visit Naples, Italy.

At Sea

As we proceeded to the western Mediterranean, I began to acquire a greater appreciation for the skill of our navy pilots and other members of the crew. I would watch the pilots with keen interest as they either departed or landed on the flight deck of their rolling aircraft carriers. These observations caused many of us to feel a tremendous sense of security. This feeling would be with me in the future when I would discover that the pilot of a commercial airline that I was flying on was a former navy pilot.

I also developed tremendous respect for many of the skilled Gunner's mates. Several of the ones on our ship came from the hill country of Kentucky, Tennessee and West Virginia. Their accuracy in the use of the big guns was nothing less than phenomenal and they would frequently receive awards for this. It would be put on display when they shot at drones or other targets.

When the blare of "G.Q., G.Q., man your battle stations; man your battle stations" which had echoed across the ship's loudspeakers subsided, our big guns would begin their roar. The Gunner's Mates on the Flagship would demonstrate that they were the best in the fleet. It was not uncommon to hear one of them make the comment:

"We can knock the fuzz off a mosquito's [expletive] at 500 yards without touching the skin if we wanted to do so."

Vancy Bulluck had attended Howard University in Washington, D.C., where he majored in music prior to joining the navy. He planned to continue his studies upon the completion of his military service. He was very mature and affable albeit somewhat reserved. He became my confidant and trusted friend. He also taught me Black History.

On those occasions when I felt as though a senior white petty officer was trying to take advantage of me, Bull, as I affectionately called him would intervene on my behalf. When he finished his tour of duty and departed for the United States to settle in northern, California, his departure was sorely missed. We communicated with each other by mail, and when I left the Sixth Fleet, I would finish my tour of duty at the San Diego Naval Training Center. I did not know it at the time, but we would see each other again and it would have a profound effect on my life.

Naples, Italy

When we arrived in Naples, Italy en route to France, I wanted to determine whether the Italian women were as beautiful and as sexy as those that were depicted in film. Visions of women resembling *Gina Lollobrigida* and *Sophia Loren* danced through my mind.

Noel Myricks

I also wondered if I would have the opportunity to see *'Lucky' Luciano*, the Sicilian Mafioso chieftain who had been deported from the U.S., and who was rumored to reside in Naples. I found Naples enjoyable even though it did not live up to my expectations.

My first experience there was being harassed by hordes of children trying to hustle me and others for money and adults peddling their goods with an intensity that I had not observed anywhere else.

On a more positive note, I had the opportunity to see *Mt. Vesuvius*, a volcano that had erupted and buried *Pompeii* in 79 A.D., and was still active. It had last erupted in 1944 and killed an estimated 3,000 people and left over 100,000 homeless. Its lava flow was over 200 yards wide. Notwithstanding this fact, the people in Naples and its surrounding towns pursued life with no apparent apprehension about any immediate eruption of the volcano. It was my hope that it would not erupt again, at least while we were there.

My first exposure to Neapolitan dining was a thoroughly enjoyable experience. I thought about the time when I was in high school and one of the white kids in the gym locker room said he was going to get a pizza pie after basketball practice. He seemed quite excited. I had never heard of pizza pie and I asked him whether it was like sweet potato pie. He responded in the negative with a puzzled expression on his face. He told me that he had never had sweet potato pie, but pizza pie was not sweet. I wondered what kind of pie could be enjoyable and not be sweet. Now, with a broader knowledge of food, other than *soul food*, that dialogue seemed to have occurred centuries ago. Shortly thereafter we departed Naples and proceeded to return to our homeport.

Villefranche-Sur-Mer

Although I had enjoyed the places visited, it was great to get back to France. While at sea, I developed a friendship with a sailor from *Spanish Harlem* whose name was *Tracy*. He worked in the Galley on the ship. He was a very handsome person with regal bearing. He had a roman nose, a tan complexion that seemed radiant at times and the physique of a well-conditioned athlete. He was a superb dancer who made a special effort to teach me some of the more sophisticated techniques in the various Latin dances which were the rage in Spanish Harlem and on the Riviera. He aspired to become a professional dancer with the Katherine Dunham dance troupe upon the completion of his military duties. Notwithstanding all of this, he was a very modest, albeit humble person.

It was not uncommon to be at a bar or club and observe women quiver when they saw him. There was an occasion when friends and I had tried repeatedly to get a certain waitress at a club we frequented to spend some quality time with us. We were unsuccessful. And then one evening Tracy, Jay and I walked in together. When this waitress saw Tracy she said to another waitress when she observed him:

"Mon Dieu" (My god). She almost dropped her tray.

She proceeded to tell her friend rather excitedly that she had to make love to him.

Jay and I looked at each other with raised eyebrows and smiles. Tracy had made no overtures at all; he simply appeared on the scene. Without hesitation, she put her tray down and asked Tracy to dance. He smiled, removed his coat and put on a show. Shortly thereafter, the waitress notified the manager that she was through for the evening and she and Tracy left. I subsequently learned that Tracy had moved in with her and she was buying him some nice French and Italian clothes and treating him royally.

I found this particularly amusing because Tracy barely knew more than 10 or 20 words of French and her knowledge of English was equally limited. Apparently, this presented no obstacle whatsoever. *-C'est la vie!*

After having been away for some time, Villefranche looked like Paradise. It served as the gateway to Nice, Cannes, Monte Carlo, Monaco, Eze, Beaulieu, St. Paul de Vence, St. Tropez and the rest of the Riviera. The colorful fishing boats of the natives greeted us; eager to take us, for a modest fee, from our ship to the dock where we would get transportation to our apartments.

I was eager to wear some of the new clothing that I purchased while away, especially my silk red and white striped sweater and white pants purchased in Naples, Italy. I also wanted to get into the pointed-toe Italian shoes and on the dance floor with them. I looked forward to strolling down the Promenade des Anglais with my sunglasses scrutinizing the beautiful women and having one of them on my arm.

When I arrived at the apartment, some of my roommates were already there. *Gary*, a fabulous piano player from California was a real class act. He spoke fluent French and was madly in love with a French girl whom he would eventually marry. He would go on to become a prominent lawyer and a law professor in one of the most prestigious law schools in the country – *Boalt Hall*, the law school at the University of California at Berkeley.

Chris, another roommate was a saxophone player who seemed to live to play jazz. He was from Minnesota and aspired to make it as a professional musician. He planned to attend college and major in music, but he would often state that the degree would simply be a security blanket. He wanted to earn his living as a jazz musician.

Then there was Michael aka *Little Jazz.*, a drummer. He was an Italian kid from *New Haven, Connecticut*. He had dropped out of high school but planned to complete his G.E.D., while in the navy. He also wanted to become a professional jazz artist. Occasionally, Michael and I would party together, but this tended to be the exception rather than the rule.

Our proprietor, *Lucien*, spoke no English at all. He owned and managed a restaurant at #6 *Rue deLille* in Nice.

The restaurant was on the first floor of his apartment building. He was a good Chef and would always serve great meals and share with us his experiences in the French underground during the Nazi occupation of France.

When Gary invited me for my first lunch, I was quite surprised at the number of different servings of food, with salad served last. When I asked for coffee, it was served in a small cup. I wondered why but did not inquire and no one said anything. I had never heard of *Espresso*. I mistakenly assumed that it was going to be similar to something like *Maxwell House* coffee. I was almost floored when I took a sip. Everyone at the table laughed. Gary smiled and said French coffee was stronger than American coffee. Eventually I cultivated a taste for it.

After having lunch with Lucien and those who I would share an apartment with, I went to a club and waited for Jay and Bob. We would frequently go there in the late afternoon. Since it was early, I decided to go to the beach. Even though it was spring the beach had many beautiful women in bikinis. While there I met an attractive young lady on vacation from Paris. Her name was *Piki*. A relationship rapidly developed and within a short period of time we were rubbing sun tan lotion on each other.

One day she took me on her motor scooter to a more sheltered inlet to swim. I had no idea that people swam in the nude at this location until we arrived. Piki took off her clothes and asked me to do the same. I was glad I had my sun glasses on to avoid people noticing that I was staring at them. I got out of my clothes and we swam in the sea. Afterwards, we went to dinner. Piki, with her green eyes, olive-complexion and bronze colored hair became the woman with whom I would spend many memorable moments. She had a girlfriend, *Francois* who she introduced to Bob. Francois and Bob would find enjoyment in the arms of each other. The sheltered inlets hidden from the public eye provided countless evenings of indescribable pleasure.

Cannes and St. Paul de Vence offered an additional variety of sights and elegant night life. Mornings and afternoons were usually spent at the beach or on tennis courts surrounded by the overhanging red-tiled roofs on the Mediterranean villas. Picnics were taken in the rolling hills of St. Paul de Vence or the perfumed plains of the city of Grasse up in the hills. The wines, especially the full-bodied red wines which were specialties of the area were like the women; rich and luxurious to the smell and taste.

I would eventually learn that even in the winter, an attractive ski resort like *Valberg,* hanging there on a mountain shelf of 5,000 feet offered incomparable experiences. I began to fully comprehend and more fully appreciate the French expression *Joie de vivre.*

There would be an occasion when I watched *Aristotle Onassis* cruise into *Villefranche* on his magnificent yacht. His speed boats were lowered and sent ashore to deliver his guests. I envied him, but I would not exchange all of his wealth for the vigor of my youth. Physically, I was in the peak of health and on the French Riviera with all that it could offer and I took full advantage of it. I could sit at the outside café of the Hotel Negresco, one of France's artistic treasures on the Promenade des Anglais and sip cognac or vermouth cassias ever so slowly and watch the beautiful people enjoy the good life. I began to have a greater appreciation and understanding of the words of the author Thomas Wolfe, who wrote – *You Can't Go Home Again.*

Tension in the Middle East

After approximately three weeks in France, our stay was interrupted and we had to go to sea again. We left at approximately 6:00 a.m. Some sailors were left behind in the rush to get underway. The Middle East had become so tense that President *Eisenhower* had ordered the Sixth Fleet to patrol the waters of the eastern Mediterranean. The spirit of nationalism and independence had spread and the peace and stability in Lebanon had been threatened. The U.S. had interests that had to be protected. At this point in my life I did not have a clearly defined ideology. All I knew was that Egypt's Nasser seemed to be the main source of trouble in that area and all reports seemed to indicate that war might occur.

We were informed over the loudspeaker that if war occurred and we lasted 48 hours, we could do the job we were sent there to do. That announcement had quite an impact on me…*IF we could last 48 hours!* I had to confront and reflect on the possibility that I could be dead in a matter of hours or at most days and there was absolutely nothing that I could do about it.

If war occurred and we survived 48 hours, we would try to get into the Atlantic Ocean and disperse. Those of us who were musicians were instructed that if we were not on duty in Flag Plot, we would be assigned first-aid duty stations to help remove injured personnel. I wanted to assist in one of the gun turrets. My reasoning was that if someone was going to shoot at me, I wanted to be in a position like *Dory Miller*, the black World War II hero, and be able to shoot back if one of the Gunner's Mates was killed.

As we cruised to the eastern Mediterranean, our main weapon in the fleet was the U.S.S. Forrestal. At that time it was one of the world's two largest aircraft carriers. I had visited it on one occasion when we had moored at sea after several exercises. There were friends in its band. I also wanted to know how it felt to be serving on a ship that looked as long as two football fields. It was, for all intent and purpose, a floating air base, which carried approximately 100 jet airplanes, mainly fighters, but some attack bombers *with nuclear bombs.*

The second carrier with us was the *Lake Champlain.* It had approximately 60-70 fighters. There was one battleship, the *U.S.S. Wisconsin* and two cruisers, my ship the U.S.S. Salem and another cruiser, the *U.S.S. Des Moines.* Eventually, we would be joined by another battleship, the U.S.S. Iowa. Also accompanying us were 24 destroyers and six amphibious ships, which had two attack personnel transports, one attack cargo transport, one landing ship dock, one high speed personnel transport, one amphibious command ship and several fleet support vessels. In addition to this there were two submarines, the *Sea Leopard* and the *Entemedor* and a Marine battalion of 1800 men. There seemed to be a feeling among the crew that we were combat-ready for any and all adversaries.

Russian Subs

While working in Flag plot, sonar data revealed that we were being followed by Russian submarines. Although it was in the early hours of the morning, information of this nature was of sufficient importance that the Admiral was awakened to come and assess the situation. He emerged, dressed in a Naval Academy robe apparently given to him by his youngest son who had graduated from the Academy the year before.

The Admiral came into Flag plot with a scowl on his face. Everyone stood up. I wondered whether the scowl was due to the fact that his sleep had been disturbed or if it was attributable to the seriousness of the situation; or perhaps both.

He looked at the sonar data and radar scope, talked to the duty officer in charge and the petty officers responsible for watching every movement of the subs. He recommended that we increase our speed to lose the subs and to monitor the situation closely and inform him if the subs engaged in any unusual behavior. When he returned to his quarters his marine guard, who was always posted outside his door, snapped to attention, opened his door and the Admiral retired for the night.

One of the things learned during this experience was that one of the tactics which Russian subs would use when they engaged in their cat and mouse games with us would be to try and penetrate our outer perimeter which consisted of smaller ships and destroyers. The objective would be to try and get under a carrier which would be surrounded by a flotilla of other ships. The top priority appeared to be the protection of the carriers.

If a sub could get under a carrier, its detection at this point would be difficult and the sub would be in a position to launch its torpedoes, with nuclear tips, at other ships while enjoying the protection of our own carrier. One of the best defenses against this strategy would be to increase our speed on the theory that a ship on top of the water could go faster than a submarine traveling under the water. The next best defense would be to warn the submarine to keep away, and if this order was not complied with, to take whatever action the admiral deemed appropriate.

There was a feeling among some of us that the admiral would not have any reservation about sending a Russian sub to the bottom of the sea if his warning was not heeded. Fortunately, by increasing our speed, we lost the submarines.

Noel Myricks

Upon arriving in the eastern Mediterranean we engaged in exercises off the Gallipoli Peninsula of Turkey. Upon the completion of these exercises, we cruised toward Beirut, Lebanon. There was an unusual air of excitement about this visit. Those who had been there on previous visits would frequently tell me:

"If you think the Riviera was nice, wait until you see the belly-dancers of Beirut." Comments such as these were a pleasant diversion from the very real possibility of a major confrontation in this part of the world.

Beirut Lebanon

It is located southwest of Tripoli, Libya on the eastern edge of the Mediterranean. It has a coastline of approximately 130 miles and its summers are long, hot and dry and its winters are cool and rainy. Lebanon became a fully independent and sovereign state at the end of World War II. *Beirut* was a city where European-style villas were numerous and beach resorts and luxury hotels were common. Western culture was woven into the fabric of Lebanese life, especially that of the French. Concerts of classical western music were performed and well-attended, especially by the well-educated upper income groups.

Lebanon in general and Beirut in particular was very different from its neighbors in virtually everything. The people referred to themselves as *Arab* and they spoke *Arabic* and adhered to the *Arab League,* however, one of their greatest historians maintained that only about five percent of the Lebanese had Arab blood in their veins.

It was a truly unique place in that it was the only Middle East state that was predominantly Christian, and the only Arab state without *Islam* as its state religion.

One reason for the tension in the area was that various rival blocs who claimed to represent the ideals of Arab Nationalism and unity threatened the balance of Lebanon's ethnic politics. Egypt's Nasser was agitating and trying to undermine the pro-western President of Lebanon, *Camille Chamoun,* who was a *Maronite* Christian.

During the period 1956-57, Lebanon was more prosperous than it had ever been. It was Beirut and not Cairo that was regarded as the Paris of the Middle East. Whatever one wanted to buy, whether it was Paris originals, Cadillac cars or cabarets which catered primarily to westerners, it was available in Beirut. Lebanon was also the land of my favorite poet/philosopher – *Kahlil Gibran,* who wrote the internationally known bestseller <u>*The Prophet.*</u>

After spending one day and evening in Beirut, when I returned to the ship I immediately requested and obtained permission to take a brief vacation there for a few days. Permission was granted. I got an attractive room in one of its luxury hotels on the *Avenue des Francais* and spent some quality time with one of the belly dancers of

Beirut and thoroughly enjoyed the various pleasures this city could offer.

When this visit was over we continued to patrol the waters of the eastern Mediterranean. After being in that area for a period of weeks we cruised to the Greek Islands of *Crete* and *Corfu*.

Crete and Corfu

Crete was one of the world's earliest civilizations and the center of the ancient *Minoan* civilization. We came there by cruising into the historic port of *Heraklion*. This was a land of legends and myths and also one of Greece's finest museums.

It produced the legend of *Icarus*, who flew too near to the sun as well as that of the *Minotaur*. It was the site of archaeological museums and the *Palaces of Knossos* that people from all over the world would come to view. My time here would be spent sightseeing and taking pictures of this beautiful island and its treasures.

After leaving Crete and spending several days at sea, we cruised to the Greek Island of Corfu in the *Ionian Sea*. Corfu was lush, green and covered with orange, olive and lemon groves. It was also a favorite playground of the international jet set. Its culture and architecture reflected the influence of its French, Italian and English conquerors.

My time here was spent indulging in water sports or touring the Island's shops and watching for the first time a Cricket match on the *Esplande*. When we returned to sea we cruised back to the western Mediterranean and to our next port-of-call, *Palermo, Sicily.*

Palermo, Sicily

Shortly after our arrival in Palermo, some friends and I went ashore. We visited the *Piazza Bellini*, the Normal palace and took photographs of the Greek, French, Spanish and *Saracen* buildings. Our day concluded with dinner at a very nice Sicilian restaurant.

Subsequent days were spent visiting tombs where bodies had been preserved seemingly intact by some secret process for generations. One of my most memorable experiences occurred on the day before we departed. While browsing in a record shop, a salesman observed the musicians lyre on my arm insignia. He smiled and tried as best as he could to confirm that I was a musician. He spoke no English or French and I did not speak Italian.

These barriers were overcome when another salesperson who spoke some English came over and served as an interpreter. She told me that the salesman was regarded as the *Milt Jackson* of Sicily; he was the best Vibes player in Sicily and was often compared to Milt Jackson of the *Modern Jazz Quartet*. He wanted to know if I could get some of my friends and return for a jam session. I agreed to do so.

I went to the ship and returned with Gary, Chip and, *Gene*, an excellent saxophone player from New Jersey. Chris came with his saxophone and *Larry*, who was from California brought his trumpet. They were joined by the Vibes man from Sicily.

Gene, who was Italian, could communicate well with them. It was a fabulous session with only a select number of guests invited by the owner of the music store.

Periodically, the owner would dart to and fro behind a nearby curtain. Gene humorously inquired in Italian what was going on behind the curtain and decided to peek. He learned that the jam session was being discreetly taped with the intent of producing a recording.

The owner seemed somewhat embarrassed and nervous. He thought we would be angry. Any apprehension disappeared after an abundance of drinks and food were supplied and the jam session continued. When it was over we bid them adieu and got into a couple of colorful buggies pulled by horses and returned to the ship and prepared to depart the next morning.

Marseille

When we left Sicily we spent several days at sea and stopped for a brief visit to Marseille prior to returning to our home port. Marseille was the largest city of Mediterranean France and the fourth largest in France itself. It reminded me of being the French equivalent to

Norfolk, Virginia, a city with too many sailors. Even worse, my street smarts caused me to feel that there were other elements present which could, in a moment of carelessness, cost a person his life. No sightseeing was done without several friends present. None of us were unhappy when we departed.

Home Sweet Home

It was summer time when we returned to France and the living was easy. The picturesque Riviera was never more beautiful. Piki was waiting for me. We spent the remainder of the day at the beach in Cannes and returned later to a Roman amphitheater ruins in Nice for one of several summer jazz festivals. Participants were, *Dizzy Gillespie, J.J. Johnson, Ray Charles, Stan Getz, Ella Fitzgerald, Miles Davis, Joe Williams* and the *Count Basie* band and others. It was a great homecoming.

Subsequent days were spent on the sandy beaches of Cap d'Antibes and St. Tropez. Throngs of people would lie mat-to-mat and under colorful umbrellas. The south of France, especially in the summer, exceeded my highest expectations. We would visit places like the Grimaldi Castle, which had been built in the 12th century. It had become Pablo Picasso's museum. It was located in a very picturesque part of Antibes. I would often find myself taking pictures of the flower stalls and quaint cafes that abounded here.

Noel Myricks

Yachts of the rich and famous seemed to be everywhere, especially in St. Tropez, Cannes and Monaco. I would frequently dine on salade Nicoise, French bread and red wine as I immersed myself in this good life as long as possible. The madness and conflict over race relations and strife in my country was an occasional item in the *Nice-Matin* newspaper. These events seemed to be occurring on another planet. France had its Algeria problem, and as the Swedish Sociologist *Gunnar Myrdal* had written, America had its *"Negro Problem"*. However, when breathing the rarified air of the French Riviera, it was easy to be naïve and fantasize about the racial progress that would occur in the U.S., when legislation such as the first Civil Rights bill in 82 years would be passed by Congress.

I was doing all I could to ignore the ugly and painful reality of racism notwithstanding my own personal experiences. I could not envision the number of people, black and white, who would eventually lose their lives or become physically or psychologically maimed for life trying to achieve equal rights for all Americans.

Palma de Mallorca

When the disappointing news came that it was time to go to sea again, it was tempered somewhat by the fact that we would be going to the beautiful island resort, *Palma de Mallorca*. This was one of the most popular vacation sites in the Mediterranean. It had quite a reputation for its Gothic Cathedral, great beaches, plentiful cafés, bars and shops and particularly its local pearls and ceramics. It lived up to its reputation.

The majority of my time was spent at two places: The *Victoria Sol Hotel*, which was the premier luxury hotel on the Island and at a restaurant/club that was simply the single most exquisite one that I had ever seen in my life. While walking around observing different places, I observed this place which was in the shape of a large boat. It perked my curiosity. Upon entering the door, I found myself in a small dark pathway approximately four or five feet in length. As I continued through some swinging doors, I entered a well-lit area where persons were sitting around a bar which was a large tropical fish bowl.

There was a beautiful waterfall behind the glass walls pouring into a body of water that flowed throughout the walls of the bar with an assortment of beautiful tropical plants and fish. After pausing and gawking at this sight, I observed another dark entrance which lead to another room where music was playing and people were dancing. After walking into this area and pausing for my eyes to adjust, I could see shadowy figures dancing slowly to music. The dance floor was marble and the ceiling was powder-blue like the sky on a clear day, with light being supplied through holes in the ceiling carved in the shape of stars. There were no visible tables or chairs.

The walls in this room appeared to be like a rock grotto, with small caves where people could sit and seclude themselves. One could see the twinkling of candle light in each cave but nothing else until someone emerged to dance or leave. The music appeared to come from a sound system hidden in the walls and the acoustics were superb. It was truly exotic.

Upon leaving, I was approached by two officers from the ship standing on the sidewalk nearby. One was the legal officer who had graduated from Harvard and the other one, who I had a cordial relationship with, was from Yale. The lawyer from Harvard asked me what my impression was of the place as they were trying to decide whether to visit it.

I responded rather excitedly and said: "It is bad; it is really bad."

My comment appeared to make the lawyer nervous.

He said "Do you mean they are fighting in there?"

I was taken aback. I wondered why he didn't understand me. The officer from Yale smiled and translated my expression in Ebonics into Standard English.

He said, "What he means is that it is a great place."

I said yeah, that's right and walked away amused that there were gaps in the lawyer's Harvard education.

I would learn in the years to come that Yale is located in New Haven Connecticut, which has a substantial black presence, as compared to Harvard, which is located in Cambridge, Massachusetts, which has fewer blacks. I surmised that this may have been where the Yale graduate learned Ebonics.

Tripoli, Libya

When we left Palma we went to sea and engaged in more military exercises, replenished our supplies and proceeded to Tripoli, Libya. This was a place which, for centuries, had served as a terminal for caravans plying the Saharan trade routes. It had also served as a port sheltering pirates and slave traders. The caravans carried gold, ivory and slaves from the western Sudan to markets in the Mediterranean area. In the 17th century it had regularly contributed men and vessels to the Ottoman fleet. Operations were conducted by pirate captains who preyed on shipping and raided the coasts of Italy to capture and carry away hostages for ransom or sold as merchandise on the North Africa slave market.

It had eventually been a colony of Italy, however, after World War II, it was agreed at the *Potsdam Conference* in 1945 that the Italian colonies seized during the war would not be returned to Italy and in 1951—the federal monarchy of Libya was born.

When we cruised into Tripoli, it was a poor and backward country which was heavily dependent on foreign aid. It had few resources and scarcely any engineers or doctors. Its major advantage was its strategic location. There was keen interest in this country by both Cairo and Moscow. Eventually, the time would come when Libya would raise a 10,000 man desert legion and a select group of its legion would be trained by British officers at *Sandhurst*, its Military Academy and at other schools for leadership roles in Libya. One of those young men would eventually become known throughout the world. His name is *Muammar al Qadhaafi*.

Shortly thereafter major petroleum deposits would be discovered in Libya and commercial development would be quickly initiated. The Libyan monarchy would soon be abolished in a *coup d'etat* by the officers trained by the British. The British had achieved some of their goals, but not in the manner they had assumed.

Bull and I decided to go into the city and do some shopping and enjoy the tourist sites. I had uppermost in my mind the incident that had befallen a sailor in *Morocco* whose body had been found floating in the river, and I was determined not to do or say anything to anyone that could be offensive.

The inhabitants appeared to be Arabs, *Berbers*, *Taureg*, Black Africans, Jews and Italians, and to a lesser extent, other people. I purchased some rugs and other objects for my apartment as well as gifts for relatives and friends and returned to the ship. The remaining days were spent doing basically the same thing and we took a short visit to the *U.S. Wheelus* Air Force base which was located there.

Caucus at Sea

When we left Tripoli we went to sea longer than usual. Our ship and other ships cruised to a small group of islands where the Admiral and other officers spent a couple of days engaged in discussions about the Middle East situation. Many of us took advantage of this brief lull from our regular routine by diving off the ship and swimming in the ocean under the watchful eye and protection of Marine guards in life boats who patrolled with their M-1 rifles in the event of shark attacks. Movies were often available in the evening at the rear of the ship.

Fall on the Riviera

Fall had arrived and my mind and heart was in France. I could hear the music of *George Shearing* or *Cal Tjader* or some Latino group singing the words *"Wa-chi Juana"* with a strong Afro-Cuban drum beat provided by someone like *Mongo Santamaria, Armando Peraza, Willie Bobo* or another fabulous drummer.

I could hear in my mind the calypso songs and melodious voice of Harry Belafonte and feel the cool night breeze caressing my face along with that of some attractive woman. Piki and Francois had returned to Paris. I was given a standing invitation to come and spend quality time with them in gay paree. I promised to do so.

Cruising into the bay of *Villefranche-sur-mer* was always an exciting event. On my first evening, Jay and I went to the Whiskey Ago-go. The Maitre d' was a young man called *Jo-Jo* and his partner was *Robert*, pronounced *Ro-bear*. We had developed a warm, cordial relationship. They greeted us enthusiastically and seemed genuinely glad to see us. We spent the evening dancing with different women and talking to Jo-Jo about the clientele present and other things of interest. When the club closed Jo-Jo invited us to go with him to a neighborhood club that would still be open and frequented only by those indigenous to the community. We were flattered by the invitation and accepted.

We got in Jo-Jo's car and proceeded to a part of Nice I had never visited. Although there was a modest fee to get in, Jo-Jo had it waived for all of us. The place was jumping and Jay and I were the only Americans there. Jo-Jo introduced us to the owner, an elderly Frenchman who I would come to know as *Monsieur Paul* and his affable daughter, *Yvette*. Neither spoke English which by this time was not a problem for me. Both were pleasant and told us that we were always welcome. Jay and I were excited and pleased that we had found a place not known by any of the persons' on the ship. We agreed not to tell anyone except for our closest friends and associates.

During one of my frequent visits to Monsieur Paul's, I met *Monique**, a university student. We danced on several occasions but I was unsuccessful in persuading her to spend the night with me. She did agree, however, to meet me the following day for lunch at one of the restaurants near the *Place Massena*. After lunch we strolled and she exposed me to a part of Nice that I had not known and a culture that had been foreign to me.

I would view the works of *Henri Matisse, Chagall, Degas, Renoir* and other artists and visit a parish where *Luther* once celebrated mass. Our relationship developed and expanded into an intimate one. Two days before my ship departed, she had to go out of town, but we agreed that she would write and we would get together when I returned.

On my last day in Nice, I walked into a bar on *Rue de France* in the late afternoon. I had been a frequent visitor and had a pleasant relationship with its owner and bartender whose name was *Morris*. When I entered I noticed that no one was there except Morris and two very Nordic appearing people. One was a blonde male and the other a stunning blonde female, with large, lucid blue eyes.

The sound of disco music was emanating from the speakers and Morris appeared to be making blatant overtures to this woman. I was surprised because she appeared to have been accompanied there by the man that appeared to be her partner. Morris greeted me gingerly, took my order, delivered it immediately and quickly returned to dance with and resume his conversation with the woman. Her partner appeared to be preoccupied with backgammon at the bar, and seemingly indifferent to what Morris was doing.

I found the situation difficult to grasp. I listened attentively to Morris' conversation and perceived that he was talking to her in broken English. I also hypothesized from her accent and appearance that she was *Swedish*.

Morris continued to dance with her; one dance after another, leaving only to go and change a record. There had been no reaction at all from her partner. Finally, my curiosity got the best of me. I walked to the bar and exchanged pleasantries with her partner. I asked where he was from.

He smiled and said, "Sweden."

I glanced at Morris dancing with his partner.

"Aren't you jealous of the way Morris is monopolizing your woman?" I asked.

I thought he might say it was his sister but he didn't.

He said rather casually, "No. We Swedes are not a jealous people. Jealously is a characteristic of you Americans."

I smiled and looked at him in disbelief. Most of the people I knew would seriously hurt someone for a woman as gorgeous as her. At that point I thought I would put his statement to the test.

I waited patiently for Morris to change the record again and then I moved quickly and asked her to dance. She agreed and came into my arms. To my pleasant surprise she pressed her body so close to mine she could feel my heart beat. She tucked her head under my chin. When Morris returned and saw this, he became livid. I could see the blood rush to his face. Nonetheless, he controlled his anger. I ignored him, confident that if he started something I could finish it.

Her name was *Zaidi**. Since Morris did not speak English that well, I felt that I had a tactical advantage since it seemed that English was a second language for her and many Swedes. Further, I had never met a Frenchman who could be more persuasive than I could in my native tongue. As we danced, I found myself becoming embarrassed because I was becoming sexually aroused and I knew she was so close that she would realize it. She did! To my embarrassment, she moved her head back from under my chin, looked at me with twinkling blue eyes and an impish smile.

She said, "Do you like it?"

For a moment I was speechless. I stuttered and blurted out the words, "I love it!"

I looked at her partner and he continued to seem indifferent as he concentrated on his game of backgammon. At this point I thought I would throw caution to the wind and take my best shot using whatever persuasive powers I could muster to get this incredibly beautiful woman in bed. I asked her to leave with me, but she was reluctant to do so at that precise time. However, she did imply that she might be favorably disposed to do so later in the evening. I was nervous. I knew that I had to return to the ship by midnight because we would be going to sea the following day.

When more patrons began to enter I found some relief from Morris. He had to serve them, but he continued to make his presence known at every opportunity. Time was on his side. Finally, the moment of truth arrived. It was eleven O'clock and she agreed to spend the night with me. I found myself confronted with a situation I had never envisioned. In the brief time we were together, she had become an obsession. I had never known anyone quite like her. I had heard many intriguing stories about Swedish women, but this was my first contact with one. I had to make a decision. Was I prepared to pay the price of going AWOL in order to make love to her? She certainly seemed worth the risk. Finally, reason prevailed.

I told her that I was in the U.S. Navy and had to return to my ship by midnight because we would be leaving in the morning. I kissed her gently on the lips during our last dance and left while I still had the strength to do so.

After that experience I became resolved to visit Sweden, the land of the Midnight Sun. The women of Sweden were the rave of the Riviera. Most of those that I saw were stunning blondes who were often accompanied by well-tanned European playboys. I decided that before I left Europe, if I had to walk, crawl or swim across the North Sea, I would get there.

As a boxing enthusiast, I read where the sparring partner of Heavyweight Champion Floyd Patterson would meet and marry a beautiful blonde Swede who had been crowned Miss World. He had met her while Floyd was training in Sweden in preparation to fight *Ingmar Johansson.*

When I talked to black sailors on other ships that had been to Sweden before they joined the Sixth Fleet, they further stimulated my curiosity by describing it as "God's Country". The time would come when I would find out how much truth was in that statement.

Departure of Friends

It had been almost a year since my arrival in Europe. I was beginning to feel like an old-timer. Within the next few months Bull and Roscoe would be returning to the U.S. When he received his discharge, Roscoe would return to the Riviera, marry the woman he had been living with and earn a living there as a professional jazz musician. *Weir*, the petty officer who I first met at music school was now a Chief Petty Officer and he would be coming to replace our current Chief.

When Bull departed, he sat in a chair aboard ship that was hoisted in the air, with a line extending from our ship to another ship at sea. As he was transported to the ship that would take him back to the U.S., the band played, *"So long, it's been good to know you."* He smiled and waved goodbye. He had been a very popular member of the band

and I'd miss him. I wondered who his replacement would be; and when I did I was shocked.

I learned to my dismay and to the dismay of some others, including our new Chief that it would be my old nemesis from the School of Music – Woody. I couldn't believe it.

I wondered if the ship would be big enough for the two of us. Woody's reputation had preceded him. In the interim, life continued as usual. After several more days at sea, we went to Barcelona, Spain.

Barcelona, Spain

Upon arriving in Barcelona, some friends and I began a sightseeing tour. We walked along the broad *Ramblas*, with its colorful flower stalls and artisan shops. The novelist *Somerset Maugham* described the Ramblas as the most beautiful street in the world. The open-air libraries and newspaper kiosks, trees, birds and flowers certainly made it attractive.

I was surprised to learn that Barcelona had its own *Arch-de-Triumph*. I was not surprised to see a monument to Christopher Columbus. We visited the *Palacio Nacional* and saw one of the biggest organs in Europe. Its collections of Romanesque and Gothic art are generally regarded as the most important in the world.

When evening came we found a restaurant on an adjacent street off the Ramblas that offered superb food and an excellent Flamenco show. Its nightclubs purportedly could rival the best of the Parisian revues. Its restaurants and Catalonian seafood were superb.

Barcelona had the well-deserved reputation of being an exciting city. I saw my first bullfight at the age of 14 when my cousin Dan took me and others to El Paso, Texas and we visited *Juarez*, Mexico. Several persons on the ship told me however, that to really see bullfighting I would have to see it in Madrid or Barcelona, Spain.

Yearly, there were more than 200 bull fights in the arenas and no less than 50 matadors, *banderillos* and *picadors*, including the most famous in the world. Barcelona had two bull-rings, *La Plaza de Toros Las Arenas* and *La Plaza de Toros Monumental*.

Las Arenas had a capacity for 15,000 spectators and La Monumental had a capacity for 19,600 spectators. It had become renowned throughout the world for the important bullfights that took place on a yearly basis. I looked forward to being a witness to the struggle for life and death between the best of bulls and the best of the bull-fighters.

Friends and I attended a bullfight at La Monumental. The stands were crowded. I was intrigued by the strut of the matadors, seemingly indifferent, but always keeping a watchful eye on *El Toro*, the bull. When the bull made its appearance there was a blare from trumpet players in the stands that pierced the air as El Toro snorting, flexing its shoulder muscles and shaking its head and deadly horns, displayed an eagerness for combat. Shortly thereafter, the fight began.

El Toro made several passes and then there came a point where the matador got on his knees, and with his sword and cape behind him, went nose to nose with the bull. It seemed to be a gesture designed to assert his dominance over the bull. There was tension and silence throughout El Monumental as El Toro and the matador stared each other down. Slowly, ever so slowly, the matador got to his feet and strutted like a proud peacock to the adulation of the crowd. This was one of the most exciting moments in this beautiful city. Eventually, the end came when the matador killed El Toro to the delight of the crowd.

Shortly thereafter we departed Barcelona and went to sea for more exercises and to make preparations for a visit to Genoa, Italy.

Planning a Party

When we returned to sea after leaving Barcelona, Jay, Bob and I spent our time together planning a private party at Monsieur Paul's club upon our return to France. We had to decide what ship personnel would receive invitations, and who would be responsible for providing the best liquor money could buy and what splendid hors d'ourves would be served. We wanted it to be a gala event, yet restricted only to invitees.

We agreed that we would finalize our plans after we got to France.

Rape aboard Ship

A couple of boatswain mates from Newark, New Jersey had their military service end and their future options severely hampered by what could only be described as an insane and inexplicable act. I knew both of them casually as a result of our mutual interest in boxing. Both were tough guys, but generally pleasant and congenial.

Often while at sea, some sailors on the ship participated in boxing in the evening and a small crowd would gather. I was an observer and not a participant, but I had gained the respect of these guys as a result of a fight I got into at sea. There was an occasion when we had stopped in the Ocean to replenish our supplies. This was done by the supplies being transported from ship-to-ship by a long line that had been shot over from one ship to our ship.

Periodically, a crate would crash and burst open and apples or some other fruit would spread throughout the deck. On one occasion, when this occurred, I rushed from where the band was performing in the gun turret to get some of the apples. While I was leaning over retrieving apples, another sailor, a white boatswain's mate leaped on my back as I was bending down. This made me angry and I pushed him off me and he swung at me. As I prepared to retaliate others quickly intervened. Nonetheless, we agreed to meet in the fantail, the rear deck area at the end of the day to finish the fight.

A small crowd gathered. This sailor was bigger and in good shape because of his duties and I knew that I was not in good shape because my lifestyle for the past year had been very sedentary. Notwithstanding this, I was ready to rumble. There were no boxing gloves, we would just fight.

When I arrived, this sailor and others were there to observe. As soon as I raised my fists, he threw a right hand that hit me in the eye and he quickly moved in to grab me around the head in a headlock and began to squeeze it. My street survival instincts came forth and I took my right hand and grabbed his genitals and yanked them. He screamed and released me. I held his genitals in my right hand and began pummeling him with left hooks. Some of his fellow boatswain's mates quickly came to the rescue and pulled me off of him.

When they released us, I put up my fists again.

"Come on, let's finish it." I said.

He held his left arm out while holding his genitals with his right hand.

He said, "No, no, the fight is over; the fight is over; the fight is over."

Others intervened and would not let us continue. Two of those who intervened were the ones who eventually got dishonorably discharged for the rape of another sailor.

Shortly after receiving notice that their orders had arrived to return to the U.S., they decided to celebrate by raping an effeminate white *yeoman* (clerk) on the ship. Predictably, he reported the rape and they were subsequently arrested and put in the brig on the ship. When we arrived at our next destination, which was *Genoa*, Italy, they were transported, under guard, along with the yeoman to the U.S. There would be a trial, eventual incarceration and a dishonorable discharge.

No one could come up with any plausible explanation for their behavior. Jay knew both of them well. They worked together although they did not socialize with each other. They had performed their jobs well and had no prior disciplinary problems until this incident. Suddenly, for some inexplicable reason, they engaged in behavior which abruptly ended their military service.

Noel Myricks

Evenings at Sea

Some of the sailors vented their energy by boxing each other in the evenings. I became acquainted with several of those who I would not ordinarily have much contact with through this mutual interest. I chose not to box except for occasional light sparring because I could not afford the inconvenience of a busted lip or worse, losing a tooth.

I had neglected my teeth as a child, and while in France I had expensive dental work performed. One of the musicians in the band, the son of a Philadelphia banker referred me to his former family dentist who resided in Monaco. This dentist was also the dentist for *Princess Grace* of Monaco. He did a superb job in replacing a partial with a permanent bridge and I had no intentions whatsoever in jeopardizing it if I could avoid doing so.

Notwithstanding this, I enjoyed watching others box. Most of them were at best only average. However, there were two excellent fighters. One was a middleweight and the other was a heavyweight. The middleweight was from Cincinnati, Ohio. I nicknamed him the *Cincinnati Cobra* after the former heavyweight champion, *Ezzard Charles*, who was also from Cincinnati. We sparred lightly with each other on one occasion and that was enough for me. He was a clean, hard puncher and when he hit someone, especially in the lower rib cage, it would make one wonder if he was getting a bone transplant. Pain would radiate throughout your body. He made me quickly realize that the sedentary lifestyle I had lived subsequent to boot camp had slowed my reflexes considerably and made me soft in areas that once were solid with muscle.

The "Cobra" frequently worked out either by punching both the heavy and speed bags or boxing others. I enjoyed watching him execute, with precision, various punches that invariably would send opponents to the canvas. He would have been at home in *Detroit's Brewster Center*.

The Cobra's partner, *Bill*, was a short, stocky heavyweight with tremendous power and precision in his punches. Physically, he resembled *Mike Tyson*. It was rare that anyone wanted to box him. Those who did would often end up battered and bloody. He had no mercy on anyone who put the gloves on; even his friend the Cobra received no mercy when Bill dished out punishment. It was hard to imagine anyone on the ship who could beat him.

One big fellow, *Bruce*, who physically resembled *"Big" Buster Mathis* since he was approximately 280 pounds decided to box Bill. He would rue the day that he did. Shortly after putting on the gloves, Bruce proceeded to attack Bill with both hands. Bill responded in kind with a vicious two-fisted assault that brought cries of excitement and anguish from observers. The volley of punches that Bill hit Bruce with literally lifted Bruce off his feet and knocked him out. I had seen fellows knocked out before but this was the first time in my life that I had been a witness to such pure, unadulterated brutality unleashed with scientific precision and devastation.

After this incident, Bill had to beg people to box him, with strong personal assurances that he would take it easy on them. On one occasion he asked me to lightly spar with him—I politely declined. I began to look forward to Woody's arrival. I wanted to arrange a boxing match between Woody and Bill before Woody learned of his reputation. That would never happen because by the time Woody arrived, the Flag had changed from the U.S.S. Salem to the U.S.S. Des Moines.

The U.S.S. Salem was returning to the U.S., and Bill, as part of the ship's crew would remain on the Salem and those of us who were musicians would be going with the Admiral to the U.S.S. Des Moines. This also meant that my two best friends and "running buddies", Jay and Bob would remain on the Salem. However, it was a matter of months before the transfer occurred.

Genoa, Italy

Genoa is the third and chief seaport among Italy's five good natural ports. It is surrounded by ancient walls. It is Italy's busiest seaport and serves the industrialized northwest part of the country. We would only spend a few days here, but they would be delightful ones. It is located on the Italian Riviera.

I enjoyed Genoa much better than Naples. My friends and I would spend our time visiting Renaissance palaces, shopping, dining and enjoying the various pleasures offered by this lovely city. We departed earlier than many had wished. Upon leaving Genoa we spent almost two weeks at sea and then cruised to our home port for the Christmas holidays.

The Rivera – 1957-58

Upon arriving at my apartment, I freshened up and donned my beret, cravat and other civilian clothes and went to greet Lucien and have lunch while awaiting the arrival of Bob and Jay. We had to finalize our plans for the party.

Lucien introduced me to another tenant in the building, *Marcel*, who was from Paris.

He asked, "Avez vous viste Paris?"

I responded in the negative and told him that I planned to go before I left Europe, but that life on the Riviera was so fabulous it was too difficult for me to leave. He said with firm conviction and resolve, that I would not have seen France until I had been to Paris. He added whatever I had experienced on the Riviera "would be nothing; nothing, in comparison to what I would find in gay paree." He stimulated my interest tremendously as a result of our conversation.

Shortly thereafter, I made plans to visit Paris in the spring. Bob arrived and told me that Jay would meet us later at the jazz club. Bob's interest in visiting Paris was also aroused when I shared my conversation with Marcel. We decided that we would take our vacations together.

After a scrumptious meal and finalizing our plans for the party, we went to the jazz club to rendezvous with Jay. Upon walking in and sitting at a table with Jay, he flashed an impish smile and asked whether we had seen the Swedes. My response was no, where are they? He nodded toward a corner of the room where two blonde Swedish sisters were talking to two young Frenchmen.

I asked how he knew they were Swedes. He said, "Look at them and listen. They're speaking English with a Swedish accent; I heard one of them tell one of the guys that they were from Sweden."

I immediately got up from the table and went over and asked *Elsa**, a lovely strawberry blonde to dance.

She politely declined and said, "Perhaps later; I'm talking at the present time." With my ego slightly bruised, I returned to my table to wait patiently for another opportunity.

After waiting for a while, Bob decided to go and ask *Annika**, Elsa's sister to dance and she accepted. It was a slow dance. Jay and I took delight in watching Bob *rap* to Annika as she frequently smiled and snuggled in his arms. After a reasonable waiting period, I decided to ask Elsa once again to dance and she agreed. I learned that she and her sister were students at the *University of Uppsala* and they lived in a small town near the city of *Falun* on the shores of *Lake Siljan,* which was roughly midway between Stockholm and *Oslo, Norway.* She was 19 and her sister was 20. They had decided to come to the Riviera for the holidays. I knew that Bob and I would make it a memorable one.

After several consecutive dances, I persuaded Elsa to tell the fellow who had brought her to the club that she and her sister would be leaving with us. She did not want to be rude, but I assured her he would understand and he did.

The evening had just begun. We went dancing at the Whiskey Ago-go and then she and I went to my apartment. Bob and Annika went to her hotel. The following day the four of us had breakfast together and planned what we would do for the remainder of the day and evening. Bob and I rented a car and we made plans to attend a party later that evening at Monsieur Paul's. It was wonderful.

Christmas was rapidly approaching. Elsa and I decided to go to the ski resort at *Valberg* in the *Provencal Alps.* Bob and Annika decided to remain at my apartment.

The trip to Valberg was an adventure unto itself. We drove in the snow along the slopes to a mountain shelf. The days were joyous and full of fun and frolic in the snow. Elsa was at home on skis where I was a novice, but a game one.

A memorable experience occurred at our first meal there. I was the only black person present, and as such, would often get more than my share of attention. By this time I had become accustomed to it. The atmosphere was such that I did not encounter any hostility nor was I made to feel uncomfortable. However, I did notice some people would strain, albeit discreetly to determine what language I was speaking so they could try and determine my nationality.

I wore no American clothes and I learned to use my eating utensils like the French. Notwithstanding all of this, my cover was blown when I received an appetizer.

While waiting to be served, I noticed that the couple at an adjacent table had received their hor d'oeuvres. The fellow at that table looked like a stereotypical Italian Count. He wore a cravat and had jet black hair that went straight back. He reminded me of a handsome and regal looking young *Bela Lugosi*, also known as *Count Dracula*.

When my eyes moved from studying his physical appearance to his plate, I observed something move in his hors d'oeuvre. As I looked closer, it seemed to be a large brownish-green snail, approximately the size of my index finger, and it was in a half-shell. The guy took what appeared to be half a lemon and squirted it on the snail, and then in one quick gesture, he picked up the half-shell and *"whish"*, he consumed the snail lying on it. I was shocked. To me, this was comparable to eating a large green worm and I could not conceive of doing that.

Suddenly, without ordering anything, the waitress was sitting a similar hors d'oeuvre on my table for me to eat. To make matters worse, when this occurred, it seemed that every eye in the restaurant was waiting to see how I would react. They seemed to sense that the moment of truth had arrived.

I quickly apologized to the waitress in French and told her that it would be impossible for me to eat this and I would not eat it. She was from Spain and did not quite seem to understand either my French or English. However, she insisted that I would enjoy it. Finally, when she realized that I was not going to eat it, she substituted a salad for the snail and I expressed my appreciation. Elsa also had a salad. Those in the restaurant who had witnessed this event smiled and nodded compassionately and we proceeded to have an enjoyable meal.

We spent three fabulous days at Valberg, often feeling that we were at the highest point in the world. We sat around a huge fireplace in a festive atmosphere and listened to the crackling logs and discussed skiing and life in general, with soft music in the background.

Upon returning to Nice, I got the distinct impression that Bob and Annika had spent the bulk of their time at the apartment, with little time or interest in doing anything else. The remaining times that Elsa and I spent together were spent dancing to the pulsating sounds of the Afro-

Cuban music at Monsieur Paul's as we celebrated the arrival of another year with friends.

When they prepared to leave, Elsa and Annika invited Bob and me to come to their home in Sweden in the spring. To our astonishment, they wanted us to meet their parents and friends and to stay at their home when we arrived. Bob and I exchanged casual glances that contained our own special message to each other as we listened to them. It was inconceivable for us to imagine a similar invitation being extended by young white females in the U.S., and having parents who would be receptive to it.

We indicated that we would come in the springtime, but tactfully suggested that they discuss the matter with their parents before we arrived, and in the interim we would write to each other. Eventually, we took them to the airport and bid them adieu.

Bob and I spent a substantial amount of time subsequent to this experience discussing, among other things, what *W.E.B. Dubois* wrote about in his classic: <u>The Souls of Black Folk.</u> We felt a twoness; that of an American and that of a black person—the desire of wanting to be perceived and responded to as nothing but a man. We realized that we had been so conditioned by race relations in America and our experiences as blacks that we decided the invitation by these young ladies was simply a manifestation of their own youthful naiveté which would be quickly addressed when they returned home and discussed with their parents. But, what if we were wrong?

We wondered whether there was really a western country, a predominantly white world where the people would respond to us simply as members of the human race; nothing more and nothing less. We would seek to find this out.

Bob and I decided that we would devote the remainder of our time in France planning to visit the land beyond the North Sea via Paris. We would take a train from Nice to Paris and after a few days in Paris we would get a train to an American Air Force base which was a short distance from Paris and then get a military plane to an air base in Oslo, Norway and then get a train from Oslo to Stockholm, Sweden.

We knew that we would have to plan carefully because the Flag would be changing soon from the U.S.S. Salem to the U.S.S. Des Moines and Bob and I would lose easy contact with each other. We agreed to meet on a specific date in the spring for our trip and we would rendezvous at the apartment in Nice and then proceed on our vacation.

Flag moves to the U.S.S. Des Moines

It was with considerable sadness when I left the U.S.S. Salem and lost contact with the many friends and acquaintances that would remain there. We had some great times together. I knew that in all likelihood, this would be the last time I would ever see most, if not all of them again. Although both ships were Cruisers, the Salem seemed *"special"* because it was my first ship and had a variety of interesting personalities.

I had cultivated a special relationship with many of the people on the ship. My locker was always well stocked with choice things to eat provided by friends who worked in the Galley as cooks. I had several friends who were boatswain's mates, the laborers on the ship. They respected me because they perceived me as a regular guy who tried to be friendly and pleasant to everyone. Many of them perceived musicians as "soft" but they knew I could fight and would if forced to do so. Thus, I was alright with them.

I thought about a young affable Italian guy, *Johnny,* who was part of the Flag crew. He worked as a janitor and lived in the area reserved for Flag personnel. He moved at ease among all of us and seemed to be liked by everyone. The time would come when we would discover that his job was simply a cover. He was an undercover agent for *Naval Intelligence.* He cultivated a relationship with the Corsican daughter of a major French narcotics trafficker. It was through these contacts that he was able to penetrate their organization and severely damage it. Some of its members were killed as a result of his work, and rumors spread that if he appeared on deck while the ship was in the harbor of Villefranche he would be assassinated.

Shortly after he completed his mission, he was whisked away under cover of darkness by helicopter to a carrier in the Mediterranean and then transported to Naples, Italy and subsequently flown to the U.S.

I would not forget the one black officer on the ship. He was young, always immaculately well groomed, pleasant and very professional in his demeanor. He did not socialize with enlisted personnel. I learned, however, that he was a graduate of *Morehouse College.* I had seen him on a couple of occasions in France with his attractive wife who was a graduate of *Spellman College.*

He was involved in an incident during General Quarters that favorably impressed me. A white officer had panicked and apparently abandoned his post. The black officer pulled his gun from his holster and told the frightened white officer that if he did not return to his duty station he would shoot him. This had a sobering effect on the white officer, who had fled along with other members of his crew under the officer's supervision. The black officer was commended by the Captain for his leadership during this very tense situation.

Return to the Eastern Mediterranean

Shortly after going to sea, Woody arrived. I recalled how Bull had assumed the role of mentor for me when I came aboard and how this gesture of friendship had made my life easier than it might otherwise have been. I decided to try and extend the same courtesy to Woody, especially since I was only one of two "brothers" left in the band. The other one was a married trombone player. He had a beautiful wife, however, he could not resist the temptations of the Riviera and eventually succumbed to them and his wife left him and got a divorce.

When Woody arrived, he did not appear to be the same boisterous, bully-type person that I had known at music school. One of the things that I told him shortly after he arrived that he seemed to pay particular attention to was that a ship could be a very dangerous place, especially at night. If he offended the wrong person, he might find that person waiting for him as he casually strolled to his sleeping quarters from the fantail of the ship after a movie. The person could seclude himself as he passed a portal and with a quick shove, push him over the side of the ship where he would become food for the sharks or torn to pieces by the propellers.

I emphasized the fact that in the blackness of the night, rescue would be impossible, and no one would know what happened. He looked at me with an odd expression on his face.

As we cruised to the eastern Mediterranean, we heard that there would be a boxing tournament in Rhodes one of the Greek Isles which we had previously visited. Ship personnel were encouraged to participate. Woody asked me to train him and we spent a lot of time together. Both of us enjoyed this activity. I told him that he had a great right cross, but no defense and no left jab. Hence, we worked on his left jab and how to hook off a jab. We also worked on defense and his tendency to drop his right hand after throwing a punch which made him vulnerable to a left hook. I agreed to be his corner man.

We did not see Woody's opponent until the first day of the fight. He was a stocky, powerfully built olive complexioned Greek with a barrel chest. He seemed to have a smile of supreme confidence. Woody had a slight height advantage, but seemed smaller by comparison. I watched with keen interest as he and Woody sized each other up.

Woody said, "That sucker looks tough."

My immediate response was, "You are going to kick his butt; you are going to kick his butt; just say that to yourself over and over. Keep that left hand in his eye every time he peeks from behind his glove to locate you; and then when he expects the left fake it and hit him with the haymaker right and everything but the shouting will be over. Make him fight your fight, do not fight his."

Fight time

The fight was scheduled for three rounds, with three minutes per round. It was outdoors in the sun and I knew it would be physically demanding and the fighter in the best condition would probably prevail. With a towel on my shoulder, I pulled the rope up for Woody to enter the ring. I recalled how T.I. Turner's words: "Stick him, stick him, keep sticking him" had been a source of motivation for me and others when fatigue had set in. The time had now come for me to be Woody's "T.I. Turner".

When the Greek entered the ring there was a tremendous applause from the local fans that had come out in large numbers to cheer their local boy on to victory. The Greek pranced around the ring waiving to his appreciative audience, bouncing and dancing as though victory was assured.

Woody seemed keenly interested in his behavior. I got between Woody to block his view and provide him with some last minute instructions. He was to avoid a slugging match initially because his opponent appeared to be physically stronger. The game plan would be to box him. Throw the jab and move; throw the jab and move. Get him to the point of expecting the jab and then begin to work combinations. Throw some feints to see how he responds. The buzzer sounded and I stepped out of the ring and took the stool. Woody was ready for combat when the bell rang.

Woody quickly moved to the center of the ring and circled his opponent. Predictably, the Greek squatted low and threw a light right hand at Woody's midsection. Contrary to the time when he fought me, Woody did not lower his guard to block the punch, but instead easily moved out of the way and countered with a light left jab on his opponent's forehead and then another one with more authority.

The Greek, irritated by the jabs became more aggressive and launched a two-fisted body attack and Woody responded with a hard right to his head and then another right. The power of those punches got the Greek's attention. He learned what I already knew – Woody could punch with that right hand.

The two fighters went toe-to-toe; each banging the other. In the fury of the exchange, Woody temporarily forgot that he had a left hand.

I began screaming, "Stick him; stick him; stick him and move; stick him and move."

Woody nodded that he heard me. He back-pedaled, pausing only to stick his opponent with hard left jabs.

I did not want to see him get into a two-fisted slugging match in the first round in the heat and have nothing left for the last round because I thought the Greek was the better conditioned athlete since Woody had been living a sedentary life aboard the ship. The bell rang ending a rather evenly matched round, with Woody enjoying a slight edge, at least in my unofficial opinion.

We discussed strategy between rounds. I told Woody to continue to box him and to refrain from going toe-to-toe until the last round otherwise he might not make it through round three. He nodded his head approvingly, nostrils expanding and contracting. He was eager to get back into combat. The bell rang and the Greek came out more aggressive than he had in the first round.

He was throwing bombs with both hands, trying to take Woody out with one punch. Woody followed the game plan. He was frustrating the Greek with jabs and right hands to the body.

The Greek, out of frustration, lunged at Woody and Woody made a spin move on him and the Greek crashed into the ropes. I cheered enthusiastically and yelled.

"Keep boxing; keep boxing; stick him and move; stick him and move."

By this time Woody was becoming more confident. He was also beginning to fight more flat-footed and becoming fatigued as the Greek was picking up the pace and pressing the attack. The round came to an end.

I told Woody the Greek may have won that round and the third round would decide the fight. The battle plan for the final round was simple. Box and move for the first minute and then when it seemed that this was all he was going to do, launch an aggressive two-fisted attack Jake LaMotta style; let it all hang out.

"Bring the bacon home" I yelled, "Bring it home."

Throw left hooks to the body and then to the head followed by a right-cross.

"Turn it on; turn it on"

I wanted him to change his style. But do not do it until I yelled because he might be too tired to finish strong.

When the bell rang, the Greek ran across the ring to get at Woody. Woody circled and moved to the center of the ring rather than succumb to the temptation of getting into a slugfest in his own corner. The Greek was throwing bombs; seeking to knockout Woody, To the Greek's frustration, Woody kept his left jab in the Greek's face and avoided his heavy bombs. With a minute and a half to go I yelled to Woody.

"Turn it on—turn it on!"

Suddenly, Woody caught the Greek with a thunderous left hook to the chest and a hard right cross to his face; the Greek was hurt. He quickly tied Woody up.

Woody struggled to free himself so he could finish the Greek off but this was to no avail. Finally, the referee separated them. The Greek's head was cleared, but by this time after those blows he had acquired respect for Woody's right hand, and he no longer pursued Woody with reckless abandon. He continued to be the aggressor, but in a more cautious manner. In the interim, Woody increased his point total with stinging jabs to his opponents face, followed by right hands that were finding the Greek's head.

It appeared after one hard right by Woody that the Greek might go down, but the bell rang and both men embraced. Woody came to the corner thoroughly exhausted. He was greeted with a cool towel and a hug for a tremendous effort.

The referee and judges rendered their decision: **WOODY WAS THE WINNER BY A UNANIMOUS DECISION**. We embraced and Woody and his opponent embraced. Other congratulations were forthcoming and the crowd provided enthusiastic applause for a very good fight.

Shortly thereafter we went to sea and continued to cruise in the eastern Mediterranean and Aegean waters for a couple of months and then proceeded back to the western Mediterranean.

I submitted my request for 30 days leave stating the countries that I would visit while on leave. A yeoman whom I did not know came to see me. He said he was processing my leave papers and he had noticed that I would be visiting Sweden. When I confirmed this, his eyes lit up and he said that the ship had been there prior to its arrival in the Mediterranean, and then he pulled out his wallet and showed me a picture of his Swedish girlfriend. She was gorgeous. And then he asked if I would give her a call when I got to Stockholm and tell her hello for him and that he was thinking about her.

I looked at him in disbelief. I could not believe that he could be so naïve. I said to myself that no one in their right mind would give another guy the telephone number of a woman this beautiful and ask him to call her. I said: "Sure, I'll be glad to call her for you." He smiled appreciatively and gave me her number.

Vacation Time

When we arrived in Villefranche, I hurried to the apartment and found Bob waiting for me. We greeted each other enthusiastically because it had been quite a while since we had been together. We decided to spend a few days on the Riviera before we departed for Paris and Sweden.

A few days quickly turned into a week. It was springtime and the beautiful women and pastel colors around us seemed everywhere. *Prince Ranier III* and *Princess Grace* had their second child and first son in March, and the festive mood was still present in April. The Cote d'Azur was magic. Bob and I realized that if we did not leave soon we would not be able to afford our trip so we boarded a train one evening and headed for the city of lights – Paris.

Paris, France

The train was crowded with students from various parts of Europe. The trip would take the entire night. There was some discussion among the passengers about the Paris police rounding up over 6,000 Moslems who were suspected of being Algerian terrorists. We were not concerned because it did not appear to have any effect on us.

Noel Myricks

When we arrived in Paris the following morning we felt an aura of excitement as we departed the train. We got a cab to our hotel in the *Trocadero* section. We decided not to contact Piki or Francois for fear that we might be tempted to remain in Paris and not get to Sweden. We proceeded down the most famous avenue in France, if not the world, the Avenue des Champs-Elysses. And shortly thereafter we saw it – the Eiffel Tower. What previously had been nothing more than a fantasy had now become a reality.

My first glimpse of the Arc de Triomphe caused me to recall visual images of Hitler's Nazi troops goose-stepping down the *Champs-Elysses* toward the Arc to the sadness of the French and countless others throughout the world. Films had portrayed tears streaming down the faces of many French men, women and children at the sight of their beautiful city being taken over by the worse mass murderer and his troops in modern times.

The *Versailles Treaty* had become a worthless piece of paper. This symbolic act by Adolph Hitler erased the treaty and whatever hopes for peace others in the world had entertained. I would periodically wonder what would have happened to me and my people if Hitler had been victorious. I surmised that once again, we would have become beasts of burden, slaves for the so-called master race. Perhaps even worse, like the Jews, Jehovah's Witnesses, Trade Unionists and others, we may have been scheduled for extermination. Bob and I were both silent.

*** Sometimes I Feel Like a Fatherless Child ***

We were in awe of where we were and what we were observing.

Upon arriving at our hotel, we quickly unpacked and proceeded to lunch at an outdoor café along the Champs-Elysses. After lunch we ascended to the top of the Eiffel Tower to get a panoramic view of the entire city. It was breathtaking. We proceeded from there to the art museum with the most complete collection of art in the world – the *Louvre*.

The Louvre had originally been a medieval fortress built in 1200. We wanted to view, among all of its masterpieces *Leonardo da Vinci's Mona Lisa*. We also were eager to see the Winged Victory of Samothrace, which had commemorated a Rhodesian naval victory at the end of the third or the beginning of the second century. We would also seek out the work of art and historical document which was symbolic of the grandeur of the first Babylonian Kingdom – the *Code of Hammurabi*.

We would look with awe at the *Venus de Milo*, which was a masterpiece from the Hellenistic period and representative of ancient art and classicism, and also view *El Greco's Christ Crucified*, *Delacroix's* Scenes of the *Massacres of Chios* and *Rembrandt's Self-Portrait*.

There was so much to see: The statute of Aphrodite, which was discovered in 1820 on the Island of Milo. Its representation of feminine beauty was a masterpiece of antique art. I had a distinct penchant for French Romanticism in paintings. The Raft of the Medusa by

Gericault was tremendously appealing. It depicted the survival of 15 people who had been shipwrecked after the sinking of their frigate, which had set sail for Senegal in 1816. Bob and I would treat our first visit as if we were sipping priceless wine that neither of us could really afford and might never taste again. We savored the moment.

We spent the remainder of the day at The Louvre prior to returning to our hotel to rest. After a few hours of rest, we left the hotel to discover Parisian nightlife. We decided that we would simply "hang loose" without making a commitment to anyone while in Paris.

We were less interested in visiting a cabaret like the *Moulin Rouge* than we were in strolling the banks of the Seine and enjoying the ambiance of Paris. We went to the Latin Quarter, with its Bohemian lifestyle, night clubs and cafés. We continued to the Boulevard St-Michel and engaged students from the Sorbonne in lengthy conversations about France's Algerian problems and America's race problems which had become of considerable interest in France when black students attempted to integrate Central High School in Little Rock, Arkansas over the objections of Governor *Faubus*. After numerous cups of espresso, we decided to call it an evening.

The following day we decided to go to a concert – *Norman Granz's* Jazz at the *Philharmonic*. The artists who were performing were *Dizzy Gillespie, Ella Fitzgerald, Gerry Mulligan, Stan Getz, Oscar Peterson* and other jazz greats.

During our remaining time in Paris we would go to the *Club St. Germain* on the *Left Bank* and spend a memorable evening there.

We enjoyed walking across the bridges of the River Seine and perusing the bookseller's stalls near the Seine and spending time in the quiet bistros of Place Pigalle. We would go to clubs in Montmarte and attend Easter Mass at the Gothic cathedral of Notre Dame and go to Versailles, the most luxurious chateau ever built by a King. We would find ourselves in the midst of all of this, speculating what we would do with our lives and whether we would ever be able to enjoy something like this again.

After several days here, Bob and I were spending more than we had anticipated. I had to sell my expensive Leica camera to be assured of having enough money to comfortably continue the trip. However, I also knew that if necessary, I could telephone relatives in Michigan, especially Aunt Kate, and money would be wired to me via American Express. Bob would also call home for financial assistance.

We left Paris and proceeded to the American military base so that we could proceed posthaste to Scandinavia in general and Sweden in particular.

Oslo, Norway

Within a few hours after arriving at the Air Force base, Bob and I were on a military flight en route to Oslo,

Norway, with a very brief stopover in Frankfurt, Germany and England. We arrived in Oslo at night and checked into the Excelsior hotel. Fatigued from the trip, we went to sleep without delay.

When we awoke the following morning, we inquired about the time differences between where we were and the places we wanted to call in the United States. Shortly thereafter, we left the hotel to go and have breakfast.

While walking down the street, we had the uneasy feeling that someone was staring at us. We paused and looked around and to our amazement several of the windows in the office buildings which were along the street were jam-packed with persons, mostly females, who were smiling and waving at us. To say that we were taken aback would be a mild understatement. This was completely foreign to our experience.

We had never experienced this before in any of the lower European countries we had visited in the Mediterranean area. It was as though we were celebrities. We smiled and waved back to all of the friendly faces and continued on our destination wondering about a reception of this nature.

After purchasing some food and returning to our hotel, we made phone calls to relatives in the U.S. for additional funds. My Aunt Kate was pleasantly surprised to hear from me. She assured me that she would wire me a few hundred dollars via American Express within the next few hours. By contrast, Bob's relative told him that no money was available to send to him, and since he managed to get to Oslo by himself, he could get back by himself. Both of us were stunned.

I did not have enough money to sustain both of us on a trip to Sweden. Yet, I was determined to go even if I had to go alone. I decided that I would loan Bob enough to get back to the apartment in France where he could be assured of room and board until he could get back to his ship. Once there, he would also be able to get an advance of his military salary from the American Consulate located in Nice.

Within the next 24 hours, the money arrived and I paid our hotel bill and gave Bob enough money to take care of his expenses and then I bid him adieu and departed by train for Stockholm, Sweden.

Stockholm, Sweden

While sitting in my seat on the train en route to Sweden, I became nervous and tried to relax by smoking a *Marlboro* cigarette. I had not anticipated making this trip alone. Bob and Jay had always been somewhat of a security blanket, and now I was alone going to a country where I would only know two people. Eventually, I dozed off.

When I awoke after midnight and looked out of the train window, I was surprised to see the sun. It appeared to be sitting on the ground a considerable distance away. I looked at my watch to be certain that I was not dreaming. The Sun was in a position that I had never seen it in, especially at this hour. I surmised perhaps that this is why Sweden has been described as the land of the Midnight Sun. I anxiously anticipated my arrival in Stockholm and finally, the train arrived.

Elsa knew that I was coming but she did not know the precise date. I wanted to be alone for a while and get a feel for the country and its people other than those whom I had met. I got a cab to the *Hotel Regina,* which was located in the center of town.

Upon entering the hotel and proceeding to walk toward the registration desk, a young blonde Swedish couple observed me as they were leaving. They smiled and said something to each other, and then suddenly, to my surprise, abruptly blocked my path.

The young man whose name was *Bjorn* said in English, with a Swedish accent, "Hi! How are you?" He extended his hand to shake mine.

I paused, shook his hand and said, "Fine and you?"

"My friend Ulla has never seen a *'Negro'* person before except in films or magazines. She would like to know if she can feel your hair."

I looked at the two of them in total disbelief. Both were smiling with the utmost sincerity and it was obvious that she did not mean to be offensive. No one had ever made such a request to me before.

She had emerald green eyes that appeared to twinkle as she looked at me. Her blonde hair was hanging just below her shoulders and her alabaster-like skin was flawless without a trace of mascara, and her smile was flawless. She had perfectly shaped full pink lips.

I said, "Sure, tell her to knock herself out."

"Pardon..?" he asked

I smiled and realized that I had slipped into *Ebonics* and he did not understand me.

I said, "Yes, she can feel my hair."

He turned and told her that she had my approval and then, in the lobby of the Hotel Regina, this woman was rubbing her hand in my hair, and then she proceeded to touch and rub my skin.

She took my hand into her own, looked at it and began to chat excitedly with Bjorn about this experience. He said she thought it was interesting that my hand was dark brown on one side and a lighter color in the palm. She seemed to be enjoying this experience and I was amused at her inspection and the delight she took in conducting it.

Finally, when she finished her inspection she said something to Bjorn and he told me that some friends were having a party that evening and he would like for me to attend. I agreed since I had made no plans.

They accompanied me to the hotel desk while I registered. I gave them my room and phone number and was told that they would come to get me around 9:00 p.m. After going to my room and freshening up, I returned to the hotel desk to talk to one of the clerks. I asked what jazz artists were in the city. He told me that Sarah Vaughn and her trio were appearing at the *China Gate* (pronounced *Sheena Gate*). He seemed to be a hip young guy and chided me about coming all the way to Stockholm to hear American jazz musicians.

We had a friendly conversation about everything from Jazz to race relations in the U.S., and where to go and what to do while in Stockholm. Eventually, I got a sandwich and returned to my room, relaxed and fought off the temptation to call Elsa and alert her that I had arrived.

Bjorn and Ulla arrived to get me at the agreed upon time. We went to a small club and joined some of their friends for the party. Everyone seemed to be keenly interested in meeting me. This was a very different experience than anything I had previously encountered in France or elsewhere. I attributed it to the fact that the black presence was not that common here.

Sometimes I Feel Like a Fatherless Child

The Swedish Experience

Many of the students were from the *University of Stockholm*; a few attended other universities. The atmosphere was one of acceptance; indeed, they seemed delighted that I was among them. This was a completely foreign experience for me and I was thoroughly enjoying it. I sat at a table with Bjorn and some of his friends, and to my pleasant surprise, attractive young ladies would come and ask me to dance.

As I watched everyone dance, I acquired an even greater appreciation and understanding of what some whites meant when they said, "Black people have rhythm."

They had a lot of energy and vitality, but the rhythmic, soul-like movements so typical of black American dance was conspicuously absent. I thought about Tracy, *Spider*, Jay and Bob; if they were here, we'd turn the place out. But no one was here but me, and I intended to do the best that I could so that the brothers would have been proud of me.

Ulla and I and others danced and then it happened. A young lady walked in that made me speechless. Although there were many lovely, indeed, beautiful women present, this one was breathtakingly beautiful. I became visibly shaken. When the song I was dancing to ended, I sat briefly and then went over to introduce myself.

Noel Myricks

I said: "Hi! Do you speak English?"

She smiled and said yes. Just at that time a ballad came on and I asked her to dance and she agreed to do so. She told me her name was *Brigitta*. She was tall, approximately 5'7, and a svelte blond, whose hair had a natural gold luster. It was hanging in front over her right shoulder almost to her navel.

She was wearing a gold necklace that lay neatly on her black chemise dress. Her shapely legs seemed to flow smoothly from the dress into her black shoes. Her large blue eyes and aquiline visage with sinuous full pink lips put me in what arguably was a hypnotic trance. Her beauty was flawless and I wanted her with every fiber of my being and I intended to use whatever powers of persuasion I could muster to have her.

When she came into my arms I became oblivious to everything and everyone around me. As I began to describe how much she appealed to me.

She smiled and said, "And I think you are a very handsome man; you have gentle, pretty brown eyes, a beautiful smile and a soft comforting voice."

I wanted to scream! Before the dance ended, I kissed her gently, but discreetly on her earlobe. She snuggled even closer.

When this dance was over, I talked about *Kahlil Gibran's* description of beauty in <u>The Prophet</u>. When I finished, her smile was even broader. We danced again, with few words spoken; none were necessary. I moved my right hand from around her waist and with an open palm placed it between her shoulder blades and pressed her even closer to me and nestled her cheek against mine. I told her that when she talked to her parents again I wanted her to express my appreciation to them for bringing someone with her beauty into the world. She smiled.

As this dance began to come to an end, I heard words come from my mouth as if propelled by some irresistible impulse.

I whispered softly – "I have to make love to you."

"I want to make love to you too." She said.

Once again, I almost screamed. At this point I knew that I would not see Elsa again; my plans had irrevocably changed and I would be spending all of my time in Stockholm with Brigitta.

We spent our remaining time at the party getting to know each other better. She was a student at the University of Stockholm, majoring in Economics. She also worked periodically as a model. The family home was in a small town near Malmo, a city in the south of Sweden.

She wanted to know if this was my first trip to Sweden, and when I responded in the affirmative. She said if I had no plans she would like to show me Stockholm and other places. I responded by telling her any plans I had would be canceled because I wanted to be with her. We both laughed. I excused myself briefly and went and politely thanked Bjorn and Ulla for inviting me to the party and informed them that Brigitta would be taking me to my hotel. They understood and smiled. Bjorn said he would call me the following day. Although I did not say so, I knew I would not be available.

We went to my hotel for the remainder of the night. The following day we had breakfast at a very nice restaurant and she showed me some of the sights of Stockholm. We went to see, *"The Divine One"*, *Sarah Vaughn* and her trio at the China Gate that night. Sarah, typically, gave a fantastic performance. The audience seemed very attentive and appreciative of Sarah's artistry. Her lilting, vocalizing and sensitive approach to melodic structure as well as the lyric content of each song, coupled with her vibrato and awesome range caused her to seem magical or as some prefer to say, "Divine." She made me feel extremely proud to be an African-American, and a member of a race of people who could produce this music in such an artistic fashion for the world. As a gesture of my appreciation for her performance, I sent Sarah a dozen long-stem roses the following day.

During my remaining time in Sweden we spent every day and evening together. Both of us seemed to have an insatiable hunger for each other. Our moments together were tumultuous and passionate. We became each other's breakfast, lunch and dinner. Brigitta had me move out of the hotel and into her apartment after my second day there. When I went to sleep she was in my arms and when I awoke she was still there.

Sometimes I Feel Like a Fatherless Child

Stockholm is a city which some describe as a city that sits on 14 islands, and for all intent and purpose *"floats on water."* We walked the cobblestone streets along the waterfront area known as *Gamla Stan* where the city's ancient roots were readily visible. We stopped for a hearty Swedish smorgasbord in one of its many restaurants and strolled narrow streets lined with houses, churches and other buildings hundreds of years old.

We cruised in a boat around the city for a more panoramic view of it. We would eagerly return to her apartment to freshen up and make love again before going to dinner. My time there seemed to pass too quickly. We visited museums and art galleries. The National Museum, *Blasieholmen* was impressive. It had on display works by the great masters from 1500-1900. At *Skansen,* I had the opportunity to see one of Europe's premier open-air museums, which is a collection of some 150 authentic houses and buildings from all over Sweden. They date to the last century or earlier.

I was shown the City Hall, where the Nobel Prize banquet is held each December and attended a theatre performance. One of the city's most spectacular attractions was the *Drottningholm Palace* which was built in the 17th century. It is known as the *Versailles of the North.* Viking art was on full display at the *Museum of National Antiquities.*

Brigitta and I invariably received curious glances by others, but not a single person was rude. There was never any indication of hostility or resentment from anyone.

Quite the contrary, I found the Swedish people to be extremely cordial and polite.

When engaged in a conversation with anyone, however, brief, the listener would be unusually attentive and genuinely interested in what I had to say. As the days passed, Brigitta and I began talking about marriage. We were thoroughly enjoying ourselves and were deliriously happy. We talked about how many children we would have and what in all likelihood would be their physical characteristics. We both agreed that they would be beautiful.

I surmised that they would probably have a tan complexion and in all probability, sandy brown hair and *"funny-colored"* eyes. Since my eyes were light-brown and her eyes were azure blue, it was assumed that since brown was the dominant gene, each of our projected three children would have light brown eyes or something reasonably close to that. She was thrilled at this description. We would laugh and agree that none would need a tan, but it would be an option which they might exercise simply to show off.

Au Revoir

When the time came for me to leave, I knew that I wanted to marry Brigitta but I also knew that my future was uncertain. I knew that in a matter of months I would be returning to the United States to finish my tour of duty. Other than that everything else was uncertain.

Notwithstanding the fact that with few exceptions, my military experience had been enjoyable. I had become a third-class Petty Officer but I did not intend to remain in the navy and I certainly did not intend to return to Michigan to work in one of the factories. The only thing I did know with a reasonable degree of certainty was that I planned to go to college but I was uncertain as to whether I would be successful.

This was yet to be determined. I was resolved to do whatever I had to do to make up for the academic deficiencies incurred in high school. But, suppose this was wishful thinking? I could not bear the thought of being a failure in the eyes of my wife and unable to support a family. These were the thoughts that were uppermost in my mind when the time came to say goodbye. I told Brigitta that I loved her and wanted to marry her, but I did not know how I could take care of her and protect her. I could not take her to America and although I loved Sweden, America was my home, for better or for worse.

She accompanied me to *Copenhagen, Denmark* I told her that I wanted to become a high school band teacher, and I planned to live in California. She was informed of my family background and that basically, I had no one to rely on except myself. She still wanted to be there for me and be a source of support, and I wanted her so badly it was painful to leave without her. Yet, I also knew that she was young and innocent, and the only thing she knew about racism and race problems in the U.S., was what she had read in magazines, newspapers or saw on television.

She had never had any direct experience with it. I could envision the pain she would experience if someone called her "a nigger-lover." She would be totally unprepared for this. It would be foreign to her experience. My fists alone could not protect her.

I told Brigitta that although I wanted to marry her I could not do it until I could be certain about my future, and when my plans became more definite we could get married. She strongly urged me to move to Sweden, but I told her that I had no marketable skills that would enable me to take care of her. This was one of those rare moments when I felt completely nude; powerless, helpless even impotent. I struggled to fight back tears and watched tears come from her eyes. Although we promised to write each other daily, both of us seemed to know intuitively that we would not get married, but neither of us could or would admit it.

Copenhagen, Denmark

Brigitta and I spent our time together in *Copenhagen* at the *Tivoli Gardens*. I told her that I expected to return to the U.S. within three to four months; however, if something occurred and I would be in Europe longer than expected, I wanted her to come to the Riviera to spend time with me. She was excited at that suggestion. Our last night together was spent as though we would never see each other again. And that was prophetic.

My plane departed the following afternoon. Prior to my departure, I escorted Brigitta to a plane that would take her back to Stockholm. Tears streamed down both of our faces as we said goodbye.

France

Upon arriving at the apartment, I was greeted enthusiastically by Bob. He had returned a week before I arrived. He told me that he had returned via Rome and had met some former shipmates. He said with their assistance, he was able to remain in Rome for about a week and had some memorable experiences to share with me. He also stated that in the week he had been back on the Riviera, he had become involved with *Josette,* a lovely young girl from Algeria. He wanted me to meet her and her friend, *Mary Louise*, a beautiful girl of French/Italian ancestry. Initially, I was not interested because of my relationship with Brigitta. He encouraged me to socialize if for no other reason than to get out of what he perceived to be my depressed mood.

Both of these young ladies were students at the University of Nice. We got to know each other and had some enjoyable times together, but the thrill was gone. My relationship was basically platonic because my mind and heart was still in Stockholm.

I wrote Brigitta daily and she did likewise. I had been instructed when granted leave to check in with the American Consulate to learn when my ship would return.

To my surprise, I learned that the ship would not be returning on the date expected.

Once again tension had increased in the Middle East and we would remain on patrol in the Eastern Mediterranean. Riots and street fighting were occurring in Tripoli and Beirut. Discontent over the government of Lebanese President Camille Chamoun had increased and the fleet had to make its presence known in that area.

Transportation was going to be provided for me to get to the ship, and I was instructed to stay in contact with the Consulate on a daily basis. After several days had passed, I was flown to Naples, Italy where I boarded the aircraft carrier, the Lake Champlain, which would be leaving shortly for the Eastern Mediterranean. Bob would be leaving also, and soon thereafter we would bid each other adieu.

Years would pass before we would see each other again. This would be in the *"Baghdad by the Bay"* – San Francisco. We would spend some quality time together and share old memories.

After several days at sea, there was a rendezvous with my ship, the U.S.S. Des Moines. A line was shot from one ship to the other, and when it was secured, a chair was attached to it. I got in the chair which was hoisted up in the air and transported across the open sea. I observed the friendly faces of my fellow band members in the gun turret waiting to greet me. On cue from the Chief, the band began playing, as a gesture to me, one of my favorite calypso tunes, the "Banana Boat Song." I waved my appreciation to them and began rocking in the chair. I was greeted warmly by everyone upon coming on board.

During the next six weeks, we remained in that area. While there I had the opportunity to visit one of the ships in the fleet which had a band aboard. While visiting them I was pleasantly surprised to see that one of my former high school bandsmen, James Jefferson, a trombone player, had followed my lead and got into the Navy music program. He learned from my experience about dealing with the recruiters in Detroit and was able to enlist as a navy musician.

When there was mail call, I always had letters from Brigitta. After reading them I invariably found myself depressed. I wanted her to be with me when I returned to America but I did not know if I could provide her with the necessary protection that she would need to survive in a racist America. And I loved her too much to permit her to be abused by those forces beyond my control.

Return to the U.S.

My orders finally arrived at the end of June. I would be going to the 60 person concert and parade band in San Diego, California. It was time to go home and pursue some dreams. I was transferred to the *U.S.S. Zellers*, a destroyer on June 18, 1958 which was en route to Norfolk, Virginia. The ship left Rhodes, Greece on June 19th and cruised toward the Straits of Gibraltar out of the Mediterranean toward the Atlantic Ocean.

I had no job responsibilities on this ship. My primary concern was trying to minimize my sea sickness because I had never been on a ship this small. Reflecting on the nostalgia of my experiences in Europe, my daydreams were disrupted by a fight on the ship. Two crewmen, one black and one white got into a fight. The black sailor got in the first blow and the fight was over shortly thereafter. This conflict appeared to be an omen of things to come.

Civil rights legislation, which had been enacted into law the previous year caused me to believe that rapid change in race relations was going to come; at least I wanted to believe this with every fiber of my being. I regretted not being able to play jazz; if so, I would have been strongly tempted to return and live in Europe, especially Stockholm or Paris. I mistakenly assumed that it would be no more than a few years before I returned to Europe. I did not know nor could I conceive of the possibility that it would be a quarter of a century before I would set foot on European soil again.

After approximately two days at sea I became sea sick and remained in my bunk for most of the trip back to the U.S. I had not been back to Michigan since I got out of boot camp in 1955; almost three years had passed.

Upon arriving in my hometown, relatives and numerous friends were happy to see me. To my surprise, many of them said that I was *"different"*. What they meant by this was that my diction and accent were different. Unwittingly, I had learned to speak Standard English and not communicate too often in Ebonics. Even strangers would periodically ask what country I was from. A change in my environment and the pressure to learn to speak Standard English in order to communicate effectively with others facilitated this change.

There were other minor but noticeable changes. While in high school, I enjoyed the large *gas guzzlers* like *Oldsmobile's* and *Buicks* owned by relatives. Now, I had a distinct preference for small, preferably foreign cars such as the Volkswagen, Renault Dauphin and the Morris Minor. I spent almost two weeks with boyhood friends and family members.

Friends and I would generally spend our evenings at places like Baker's Keyboard Lounge listening to the sounds of *Miles Davis* or *Chico Hamilton*. Prior to going on active duty in October of 1955, I had heard Miles with *John Coltrane* and *Paul Chambers*. That evening had been an unforgettable music experience. I tried to spend as much quality time with my friends as possible because I knew that in the future, I would rarely return to Michigan except on special occasions.

One of my closest boyhood friends, Adam, who had been my high school class Salutatorian held a nice welcome home party for me. He had an apartment on Dexter Boulevard in Detroit. The party was well attended, especially by some of my former girlfriends. However, there was one young lady at this party who was very lovely and appealing in an unusual way. She had an aura about her that defied description. After introducing myself, I asked her to dance. She told me her name was Tynetta. She was a superb dancer and uncommonly feminine and quite different from anyone I had ever known. She had come to the party with some friends.

One thing that got my attention about her was that she wore no lipstick and had on no mascara; her beauty was simple and pure. As we danced and talked, the quality of her mind became compelling; I could not leave her alone. I asked if I could take her home, but she politely declined. I persisted to no avail. I asked if there was someone else in her life and she responded in the negative. I asked if she would have dinner with me the following day, again, she politely declined. I was flustered. I had never experienced rejection like this. I laughed and asked whether I had halitosis, she smiled and said no.

And then she stated, "I'm a *Muslim*."

Puzzled by her comment, I said, "So? I'm a Catholic."

She smiled and glanced down.

When the party ended, she departed with friends. I did manage to get her phone number. The following day we talked and I sent her a dozen long stem roses with a plea to have dinner with me. All of this was to no avail. Shortly before my departure for California, I had even offered to become a Muslim in a last ditch effort to break the barrier between us, but time was not on my side.

California Here I Come

Shortly after arriving in California, I would periodically read articles that *Tynetta* had written in the Muslim newspaper, <u>Muhammad Speaks</u>. I would never see her in person again. However, one day over a quarter of a century later, I visited the Pyramid bookstore near Howard University in Washington, D.C. While browsing, a video tape was being played of the Muslim Convention that had been held in Atlanta, Georgia. When one spellbinding orator had finished, the host, Minister Farrakhan, introduced the next speaker. I heard him say that our next speaker will be "Mrs. Tynetta Muhammad; the wife of The Honorable Elijah Muhammad." It was Tynetta! She looked like royalty; life had been good to her.

With the exception of the very negative experiences I had in boot camp, my overall naval experiences had been quite good. However, there were occasions when I would find myself one step from disaster, but somehow would manage to survive.

Within a week after I had arrived in the U.S., President Eisenhower decided to send more than 5,000 Marines into Lebanon, many were from the Sixth Fleet, including the entire Marine contingent on my former ship. Air and sea support was provided by the Sixth Fleet.

The Iraqi monarchy had been overthrown by a group of Army officers who had formed a Republic. This revolution and the emergence of rival blocks which claimed to represent the ideals of Arab nationalism and unity threatened the balance of Lebanon's ethnic politics. The Muslim faction with the support of Egypt's Nasser was apprehensive that the pro-western President *Camille Chamoun*, a *Maronite Christian* would defy the Constitution and seek a second term—the result was a small scale civil war.

Eventually, 14,000 Americans would occupy strategic areas of Lebanon. Fortunately, no confrontation other than a war of words occurred. A new Lebanese President would be elected in September and all U.S. and British forces would be withdrawn by the end of October. All I could think of was that it would be a long time before my friends would return to the Cote d'Azur and their families and girlfriends. And some, if combat occurred, would not return at all. Whew! I was glad to be back in the U.S.

My return provided me with the opportunity to reflect on and process my experiences to date. I had been given the opportunity to develop my music skills to the fullest extent possible at the Naval School of Music. I had been given the opportunity to go places and do things that had generally been reserved only for the very rich and famous. Now with one year remaining in the service, I was given the opportunity to go to the one state I had always wanted to visit – California.

Physically, I was the same person. Mentally, I was different. There had been a substantial change in my intellect and self-concept. My horizon had been expanded in an immeasurable way. The most notable change was an attitudinal change toward education. Now I had a hunger and an appreciation for a formal education that had previously been non-existent during my elementary and secondary school years. I looked forward to the challenge ahead with unbridled enthusiasm.

When my plane descended in San Diego in August, 1958, my initial impression of my new home was that it appeared to be what I had envisioned. There were streets lined with palm trees, red-tiled roofs somewhat reminiscent of the houses on the Riviera, except these houses had a distinct Spanish and/or Mexican flavor. There was Coronado Island nestled between the San Diego Bay and the Pacific Ocean. Several of the houses had swimming pools notwithstanding the presence of the Pacific Ocean a short distance away. Military ships out in the bay got my attention as well as the private yachts, cabin cruisers and other boats glistening in the golden California Sun.

Shortly after my plane landed, I got a cab to the Naval Training Center and reported to the Musician's barracks. I would be greeted by several old friends from the Music School. Phil, an excellent trombonist and First-Class Petty Officer, who was trying to overcome various obstacles and become the first Afro-American Chief Petty Officer in the musician ranks was there. The immensely talented Steve Griffin was also here. He would meet a young lady from Mississippi, "Pete", a Wave, who would become his wife. San Diego would become his home until he retired from a very successful military career.

Paul Humphrey, a drummer was here. After several years in the Navy, he would become an internationally known jazz musician.

It was through these contacts that I met Sy Rainey, a Chief Petty Officer in the personnel field. He was an outstanding jazz pianist from Harlem. After his duties as a personnel officer during the day, he would perform at local jazz clubs in the evening.

He became my closest friend. His greatest jazz influence was Errol Gardner. Often if a person did not know otherwise and shut their eyes, they would assume that it was Errol Gardner performing. He had this lagging beat as a means of building tension in a jazz performance and would invariably surprise his audience with something that was not anticipated in his own inimical way. He could quickly move from a rhythmic attack on a song to one of regal beauty with awesome power. We enjoyed each other's companionship and would spend many evenings together, especially on the weekend.

Virtually every weekend would be spent with a female friend at the club where Sy was performing.

Afterwards, a small group of us would go to Tijuana or Ensenada, Mexico and party until dawn.

Sy and I were both men in pain although we never said this specifically to each other. We used each other to comfort and console the other by being good listeners, and offering occasional advice. He was always there when I needed him to discuss my female woes. Sy seemed to get a vicarious thrill at my bon vivant attitude and the freedom that I had as a single person. He seemed to particularly enjoy observing me pursue a hedonistic life to its fullest without imposing limitations on myself because of my race. If a woman was attractive to me, I regarded her as fair-game and more often than not, I was usually successful in my pursuit.

Sy was a career Navy man with a lovely black wife. They had four lovely, vivacious daughters. Sy and his wife, *Marie** married when they were teenagers. He loved her, yet, he also loved Marcia, the sinuous and seductive white southern wife of a white career Navy man. Marcia also loved him. Sy loved Marie as his wife and mother of his children. She had been his Rock of Gibraltar for the family over the years during both tranquil and turbulent times. However, Marcia was like an addiction to him. He would often tell me that when she walked into the club where he was playing, as soon as he saw her he would get sexually aroused.

His nostrils would widen in an almost animal-like fashion when he spoke of what it was like to make love to her. He would remark that she was the blood in his veins and the air in his lungs. He felt pure, unadulterated passion.

His smoking and drinking would often increase when he spoke of her; especially her legs and how her body would quiver when they made love. His music would acquire a fiery and passionate quality, and then suddenly, the mood would shift to one of tenderness and longing. When he would take a break after a song, he would often ask me: "Did you hear me make love to her with my music?" More often than not, I would respond in the affirmative, and add: "So did Marie."

His expression would quickly change to one of surprise, embarrassment and sorrow. He did not want to hurt Marie, but he was obsessed with Marcia

Afterwards when he went home with Marie, he would immediately rush to a bedroom where he had some privacy, close the door and call Marcia so that he could hear her voice once again and share one more intimate moment together.

Eventually, it became sad to observe. I cared deeply for both Sy and Marie, and I could witness their respective pain. Marie was keenly aware of the romantic attachment Sy had for Marcia; yet, she said nothing. However, on one occasion, she told me that she wished Sy would make a decision as to who he wanted to spend the rest of his life with; that she was still young and attractive enough to have options. I simply listened without comment. I could see the pain in her eyes. However, on one occasion, without elaborating I did suggest that I thought it would be good for both of them to talk to a Marriage Counselor or Family Therapist.

Marcia eventually got pregnant by Sy. When the child was born, it was dark-complexioned and resembled Sy. It was embarrassing for everyone. Initially, Marcia's husband tried to hide his pain and accept the fact that he was not the father of his wife's child. However, this harsh reality became so painful for him that he divorced Marcia. Sy's initial response was to increase his smoking, drinking and anxiety.

Marie seemed to be a woman who wanted to hold her family together, and at the same time she wanted Sy to tell her what he planned to do about the relationship that had put such a strain on their marriage. Marcia waited patiently; she knew that she had Sy's baby and his mind, and that eventually she would have him. It was simply a matter of time. This turned out to be true. Eventually Sy left Marie and married Marcia.

Notwithstanding this seemingly carefree and hedonistic lifestyle, I never lost sight of my priorities. I enrolled in the evening program at San Diego Junior College. By the time my tour of duty was up, the grades that I had earned were good enough for me to be accepted to the University of San Francisco.   My remaining time in San Diego was devoted to my military duties during the day and my academic endeavors in the evenings. When time allowed, I was involved in some recreational activities, especially baseball. As a result of this, I kept a

Louisville Slugger baseball bat in my barracks locker. This simple fact saved my life.

One Saturday when I returned to the barracks in the afternoon to change clothes to go out for the evening, one of the career bandsmen, an alcoholic, without any provocation began cursing at me when I entered the building. I was taken aback. Until this incident our relationship had always been cordial. I was bewildered. To the best of my knowledge I had never done anything to him or said anything about him that was offensive.

Apparently, a woman with whom he was involved had canceled a date with him, and by some strange figment of his imagination, he decided to blame me for it. I did not know his woman and to the best of my recollection had never spoken to her.

I just happen to be in the wrong place at the wrong time. When he began to make false accusations about me being interested in her, I told him in no uncertain terms that I did not know her nor would I be interested in her. That set him off.

Suddenly, he yelled, "Pretty Boy, I'm going to cut your throat!"

He pulled a switchblade knife out of his pocket, pushed the button and when the blade popped out, he charged toward me.

I fled upstairs to my locker, snatched my baseball bat out and got in a position which indicated that I was ready to hit his head as though it was a baseball. When he got to the top of the steps to find me, he saw that I was waiting on him with ill-will in my eyes. He quickly turned to flee down the steps but it was too late. I hit him with the bat between his shoulder blades and he dropped the knife. He continued to run and I continued to hit him in the back and on his arms and legs. I hesitated to hit him in the head for fear that I would kill him. He stumbled and fell to the floor, with one arm up in front of his face and begged for mercy. I stood hovering over him with the bat. I told him again that I did not know his woman; had never talked to her and if he ever threatened me again, I would kill him.

"Do you understand me; I will kill you [expletive] do you understand that? Don't ever mess with me again." I yelled.

As I began to walk away I told him that he had better work out whatever problems he had with his woman before he got himself killed messing with the wrong person. I retrieved his knife and broke the blade and discarded it. He got up and hopped slowly back inside. He thought his ankle was fractured but he only had a sprain. He kept his distance and never bothered me again during the remainder of my tour of duty.

San Diego Community College

I enrolled in evening classes at San Diego Community College shortly after arriving in San Diego. En route to my classes one afternoon, I stopped by a confectionery located on Broadway in the downtown business area of San Diego. I wanted a candy bar to snack on before I went to class. *Jill**, was a vivacious, attractive young Jewish girl who worked there part-time while pursuing her degree at San Diego State College. We talked and she agreed to have dinner and attend a jazz club with me.

When we met the next day outside her place of employment, she greeted me with a big smile and we held hands and walked away. We had an enjoyable evening together and agreed to date again. I received a telephone call from her the following day. Her employer had called her and told her that she was fired because she had been seen holding hands with me by someone who worked in the building. She said the person who reported her was one of the businessmen. He was from Mississippi. She knew him and her employer told her that he demanded that the employer fire her. I was speechless.

I cursed myself for being so naïve as to think that California was somehow different; that I could behave in California as I did in Europe without any dire consequences. I wanted to console her, but instead, she consoled me.

She was from a middle-class home in the El Cajon area of San Diego. Her mother was a teacher who lived in a very comfortable and attractive upper middle-class community. Jill stated that her job was inconsequential and that she would not have any problem getting another one. And then she looked at me and said that she simply wanted to be with me and wanted me to love her. Momentarily, I was at a loss for words.

We met later than evening and drove to the coves of beautiful *LaJolla* (pronounced: *La Hoya*); a place some consider the Monte Carlo of California. We made love under the moon light to the rhythmic and melodious sounds of the Pacific Ocean caressing the shores. All problems seemed to disappear.

Our relationship developed. When I walked close to her and held her hand, her body would break out in goose pimples. She had a tenderness about her that was indescribable. One day she told me that her mother wanted to meet me. I was surprised that she had discussed me with her mother.

She took me to the family home and we had snacks and spent a pleasant evening together. Initially, there was some uneasiness on my part, but I tried to conceal it with humor. Her mother made me feel welcome and I appreciated this. The letters between Brigitta and I had become less frequent and although we would correspond with each other on special occasions, such as Christmas, eventually they stopped altogether. Our lives were going in different directions and we were simply too many thousands of miles apart. Jill did her best to fill that void in my life. She often made me feel as though I was 20 feet tall and the most important person in the world.

She would go to Tijuana with me, Sy and other friends, and she let me know in no uncertain terms that she wanted to share my life, married or unmarried. I felt undeserving of such tremendous love. I was too frivolous and did not want to hurt her but eventually I did.

While performing with the Naval Training Center band at a weekly boot camp graduation, a beautiful tan Wave who resembled the actress Dorothy Danridge caught my eye. She was stationed on the base. As soon as the graduation ceremonies were over, I sought her out and introduced myself. Her name was Marilyn*. I became captivated by her. We had a torrid relationship for approximately three months and it came to a sudden halt because both of us were two egocentric persons.

Then there was Alice, a beautiful Hawaiian. When we attended a concert by Stan Kenton, every eye in the room seemed to be on us. Her creamy complexion, liquid brown eyes and soft, silky black hair seemed to radiate throughout the room. This relationship lasted for a few months but never developed into anything of substance.

The highlight of my experience with the San Diego band occurred when the band received an invitation to come to Burbank, California and perform on a nationally televised *"Victory at Sea"* program with the movie star, Jerry Lewis. This was a wonderful experience. I had the opportunity to socialize with the World War II Pin-Up Girl, Betty Grable and her musician husband, Harry James as well as Jerry Lewis and other celebrities.

Reconnecting

One afternoon I received a surprise phone call from my homeboy, *Charles Anderson*. He had joined the Marine Corps after dropping out of high school and was sent to Korea. We had communicated with each other for a while and then he suddenly stopped writing. Thus, I was surprised when he contacted me. He told me that he was stationed nearby at the Marine base, Camp Pendleton. We got together the following day and shared our military experiences. Discharge for both of us was rapidly approaching.

Charles had always been special to me. He had been my first best friend. As youngsters in elementary and junior high school we would explore the world together. We had tried unsuccessfully to catch the northern pike and had hunted pheasants and rabbits together. We had spent countless hours honing our boxing skills and living vicariously through our heroes such as "Sugar" Ray Robinson and the *"Hawk from Havana Cuba", Kid Gavilan.*

Between the third and 10th grades, Charles and I would box each other and we both knew that I could beat him. However, as we grew older and focused more on developing our skills as boxers we rarely boxed each other.

One day, to my surprise he said to me, "Let's spar."

I looked at him, somewhat in disbelief and said, "Are you serious? Do you *really* want to spar with me?"

He smiled and said, "We'll have a light workout."

I said okay. So we went to our mini-version of Madison Square Garden, a place where many of the kids in the neighborhood came to test their boxing skills – his basement at 408 Campbell. Battles had been waged there as we tested our manhood.

After putting on our boxing gloves, we were having a light workout and then, once again to my surprise, Charles said: "Okay, let's heat it up."

My response was: "Do you really want me to go into my Jake LaMotta act with you?"

A guarded smile came across his face, and he nodded his head in the affirmative.

What I didn't know but would soon find out was that while I was going to try to act as though I was Jake LaMotta with him, he was going to act as though he was Sugar Ray Robinson with me. I came at him swinging both fists, and before I knew it, I was hit flush on the chin with a right hand that caused me to see all kinds of colored stars. A paralysis began to set in my legs, and as an act of desperation, I lunged forward and tied him up while I tried to clear my head and figure a way out of this situation without losing face. Suddenly, there was a voice emanating from the kitchen upstairs. It was the voice of his mother yelling for him to come to dinner.

I immediately broke the clinch and began taking off the gloves while encouraging him to go to dinner. He looked surprised and suggested we continue a little while longer, but I said no, he had to go eat. I promptly went home to think about what had happened.

The next day I asked him what he had been doing for his boxing skills to develop so well. He smiled and confided in me that he had been going to Detroit's Brewster Center, a place where the legendary Brown Bomber, Joe Louis had trained as a youngster. Charles honed his skills there and had not told me or anyone else.

He subsequently helped me to refine my skills and in my last formal fight in high school, I won the championship in my division and Charles won it in his and earned a trophy as the best boxer in the tournament.

At one time, Charles and I participated in the school music program together. Charles played clarinet and I played the trumpet. Eventually, Charles discontinued his music studies so that he could participate more fully in athletics. He did this until he dropped out of high school.

Now, years later, with Charles completing his tour of duty in the Marine Corps and me completing my military service, I asked why he quit communicating with me. He said that my postcards and letters caused him to become depressed. He added that while I was describing the enjoyable experiences I was having in Europe, he was patrolling the DMZ in Korea fearful that a North Korean soldier would shoot him without provocation at any given moment. He added that they would frequently point their rifles at him as a form of intimidation. Eventually, this caused him to have a nervous breakdown.

When I inquired about his plans after he got out of the Corps, he was uncertain other than he planned to return home, get his G.E.D and learn a trade. When we were in high school, he was the best boxer in our school. I asked whether he had pursued his interests in boxing in the Marine Corps and he responded in the affirmative. While in high school, there invariably were glowing comparisons between his skills and those of the great Sugar Ray Robinson.

I told him that I felt he had the talent to become a world champion, and with the proper training and management he could achieve that goal. I added that I had met the former manager of *Archie Moore*, who reigned as Light Heavyweight Champion of the world longer than any other light-heavyweight. When Moore retired, he bought a ranch in the San Diego area. His former manager owned a jewelry store in San Diego. I inquired whether he would be interested in meeting him with the idea of getting him as a manager and perhaps Moore as a trainer. He said: "Sure! Hook it up."

En route to class the following day, I stopped by the jewelry store and told the owner about Charles and his boxing prowess. I described him as having a boxing style very similar to Ray Robinson and felt that he could be a future welterweight or middleweight champion. The owner asked me to bring Charles by the store. I was excited. I called Charles shortly thereafter and arranged for the two of us to meet with the owner.

When we met with the owner we were greeted warmly. One of the first things the owner did was to take the right hand of Charles in his own and examine it. Then he discussed Charles boxing experiences both in high school and the Marine Corps. He wanted to know whether Charles would be more comfortable fighting as a welterweight or middleweight. They appeared to have good rapport with each other, and the manager was interested.

And then he said to Charles: "Why don't you meet me here Saturday morning and we'll go out to the *salt-mine* where Archie trains and the two of you can spar with each other and I can see what you've got. If you're as good as Noel claims, I think we'll be able to do business together."

The "salt-mine" was a 120 acre ranch owned by Moore which was euphemistically referred to by that name. Charles' eyes got wide-open.

He said, "Archie. You mean you want me to spar with Archie Moore?"

The owner responded in the affirmative reiterating that he wanted an opportunity to assess Charles skills and also get the benefit of Archie's opinion. Charles agreed to return but I could detect that he was apprehensive.

When we left Charles expressed his apprehension to me about sparring with Archie Moore. I made the argument that at this point in his life, Charles was in superb physical condition and Moore, in boxing terms, was an old man. Further, Charles knew Moore's style; we had studied him countless times, and if he impressed Moore and his manager, he could have a great shot at becoming a world champion. Charles agreed that we would meet at the store at 9:00 a.m. on Saturday. I was excited; one of my best friends was about to launch a professional boxing career. I knew that when he did everyone in our community would either be in attendance or in front of a television set.

I could barely sleep the Friday night before we met. To say that I was excited would be an understatement. I truly believed that Charles had the potential to be a world champion, and I was looking forward to seeing him spar with the great Archie Moore.

Charles would have not only youth on his side, but a height advantage and speed, and I knew that he would know how to use those to his advantage. The old mongoose, as Archie was affectionately called would have his hands full with this young tiger that was as smooth as velvet. I tried to allay Charles concerns by pointing out that Moore would not be the same man we had observed on numerous occasions when we watched the Friday night fights. He was close to 50 and wouldn't be able to touch Charles.

I stressed the fact that we had studied Moore like a book we had read a thousand times; we knew what he was going to try to do and how he was going to try to do it whereas Moore knew nothing about Charles. He gave me a blank stare which I could not interpret but I could see self-doubt in his face. I realized once again that I had more confidence in his abilities than he had in himself. That disturbed me. I had seen this expression in his face before when he had to fight someone in our high school boxing tournament from a neighboring community whom he knew nothing about. His last opponent had charged across the ring to proceed a relentless two-fisted attack. Charles quickly tied him up, moved to the center of the ring where he could maneuver and then began to stick his opponent with rapid left jabs followed by jolting right crosses and an occasional uppercut that had his opponent in trouble round after round.

Once Charles got his opponent in a corner everything was over but the shouting. Left hooks and right crosses zinged off his opponent's head like bass drum mallets off a bass drum. His opponent went down and got up at the count of eight. Charles methodically moved in for the kill with other devastating punches and the fight was stopped. Charles had won by a technical knockout. When Charles and I discussed the fight he said that his opponent had scared him when he charged across the ring throwing punches that seemed to go at the rate of a mile a minute, and he felt that he had to fight for his life. This was the Charles that I wanted Moore's former manager to see.

When Saturday morning arrived, I was at the store early. When 9:00 arrived, Charles did not appear; then it was 9:10, and there was no Charles. Finally, out of frustration, I wondered how he could have overslept on an occasion like this. I called his barracks and asked to speak to him. The person who answered told me that he had left to go home to Michigan the previous day and that a friend had driven him to the airport. I was shocked. He had not bothered to call to inform me of his decision.

In the years to come when I had to go to my hometown for a funeral, Charles and I would get together. Basically, he told me at that time in his life, he could not envision himself getting into the ring with Archie Moore; he didn't care how old Moore was; he could not envision himself boxing him. All I could say was that I had more confidence in his ability than he had in himself. I added that if I had his ability, I would have had to find out how far that ability could take me.

He had second thoughts about that decision in the future but it was too late. He also continued to suffer from the mental disability he incurred in the Marine Corps which would periodically result in him being hospitalized or incarcerated for short periods of time. And there were problems with drugs and alcohol and he lived at the family home. His sole income was from Veterans benefits since his illness appeared to be related to his military service and he was unable to hold a steady job.

A few years later I received a telephone call I had not anticipated. One of his four brothers called to inform me that Charles had been killed in jail. He had been put in jail for disorderly conduct and he was put in a cell with an inmate who had informed all who would listen that he would kill anyone put in the cell with him.

When Charles was put in the cell, this inmate attacked Charles and Charles proceeded to punch him out. Later that night while Charles was sleeping, that inmate took a pillow case and choked Charles to death. I spoke at his funeral and saw my friend for the last time. During the latter part of his life, he seemed to reflect on dreams that had gone unfulfilled. When we last talked he had come, at my request, to Columbia, Maryland where I was living at the time to go with me and another friend to Madison Square Garden to see Muhammad Ali and Joe Frazier fight. His remarks would often be characterized by statements such as,

"What if I had remained in San Diego and sparred with Archie Moore. . ."

And how his life might have been different.

San Francisco

En route to Oakland to attend Bull's wedding, the plane landed in San Francisco. My first visit to San Francisco was thoroughly enjoyable. I was overwhelmed by its beauty, charm and cosmopolitan atmosphere. This city seemed to have electricity in the air.

I arrived in the late afternoon, rented a car and turned on the car radio. I heard a local D.J., talking about

San Francisco as if it was a woman. This was intriguing. As evening approached the D.J. said:

"As the mist comes in off the bay caressing Nob Hill ever so tenderly, it is time to say goodnight San Francisco, goodnight."

I drove around the city to get a better feeling for it. I visited China Town, the Marina, the Fillmore and Haight-Ashbury, Nob Hill and then its Crown Jewel – North Beach. It reminded me so much of Europe. The era of the Beat generation was coming to an end, and the counter culture of the sixties, with its Hippies and Flower Children was arriving. People were sitting around tables at outdoor cafés sipping espresso coffee, wine or cognac and engaged in animated discussions. Interracial couples were walking hand-in-hand, pausing periodically to kiss with seeming indifference to the world around them. Their attire, especially the numerous berets was reminiscent of Paris.

Eventually I went to Oakland and got with some old navy friends. Some of us returned to San Francisco to partake of the night life. The sounds of jazz emanated from clubs like the Blackhawk and the Jazz Workshop. *Cal Tjader*, with *Willie Bobo* would be coming to the Fairmount Hotel. I heard Afro-Cuban sounds coming from the Copacabana and I stopped the car; parked illegally and ran into the club to see what was going on. I saw people doing the mambo, the meringue and the Cha-Cha with total involvement in their dances. I had not seen anything like this since Europe. It was exhilarating.

I had heard many favorable comments about San Francisco, but nothing had prepared me for what I was experiencing. Openness and tolerance that I had never experienced in America seemed to permeate the atmosphere. Further, the unique people and sheer physical beauty of the city caused me to be awestruck.

After the wedding the following day, a female companion and I returned once again to San Francisco. We soaked up the amenities of the city: Ferlinghetti's City Lights bookstore; the Hungry I, the Iron Horse restaurant, and of course, we danced most of the night at the Copacabana. I was in my world and could not wait until I returned to live there.

Return to San Diego

When I left for San Diego the following day, I knew that I would be attending college somewhere in the San Francisco Bay area. The only uncertainty was which college or university would I attend. I got a part-time job as a waiter/janitor in the base commissary to supplement my military income. I severely restricted my night life, saved my money and looked forward to my discharge so that I could begin a new phase of my life in San Francisco.

Sy and I still spent quality time together on weekends. My last memorable date occurred when Nina Simone came to town. A friend and I attended her performance.. She was more than a mere entertainer or musician. She was truly an artist in every sense of the word. She was a painter of moods and emotions that gave a special dimension to life. She seemed to have the capacity to reach into one's soul and articulate the most unspeakable thoughts. *"Lady Day"*, the incomparable *Billie Holiday* had died in July 1959. For me, only Billie and Nina could give the song *Strange Fruit* its special meaning when the words . . .

"Blood on the leaves and blood at the roots . . .black bodies swinging from the trees . . .burning flesh" were sung.

San Francisco – Dreams to be fulfilled

Shortly after receiving a letter of acceptance to the University of San Francisco, I requested and received an early discharge. I did not know much about USF other than the fact that it was a Jesuit institution and the university where basketball greats, Bill Russell and K.C. Jones had played and won two NCAA championships. That was enough to influence my decision to go there. I did not know that neither had received their degrees from USF and that Bill Russell would not have too many complimentary things to say about it in the future. I would learn within the year that it would be one of the biggest mistakes I had ever made in my life. I would arrive as a person who had converted to Catholicism and leave as an Agnostic. Many years would pass before I embraced Christianity again.

Shortly after arriving at *USF*, I went to the housing office and learned of the availability of a room in a private home within walking distance from the university. I investigated and rented a room until I could find better accommodations.

After unpacking I returned to the university to socialize at a party for freshmen and make some friends. To my surprise, there were no more than two other black male freshmen and no black females. Overall, there were a small number of black males, most of whom played basketball and no black females. Although everyone was polite, there was little social interaction between those of the opposite race. Most of the white kids were in the age range of 17 and 18 and of either Irish or Italian ancestry whose main interest seemed to be how their high school basketball teams would do that year.

There were few white females, with the exception being those who were studying nursing. The sister school, called Lone Mountain, was for girls, the overwhelming majority being white girls, and from what I could tell, there was not much social interaction with the students at USF. The chilly atmosphere at the party did not lend itself to asking a white girl to dance. The friendly warm faces that I had experienced in Europe were a thing of the past.

My friends were comprised exclusively of the black students. One in particular, Ken, was a senior whose home was in Oakland. We quickly became good friends and he had a car and would often take me to the University of California at Berkeley where the atmosphere was totally different and much more enjoyable.

Noel Myricks

I acquired part-time jobs as a library assistant at the Chinatown library on *Powell Street*. The Powell Cable Car was my mode of transportation to and from work. I also gave private music lessons on Trumpet and French horn to students at one of the local high schools on Saturdays. Eventually, Ken got me a better paying job as a Transit Clerk at one of the local banks. I remained there until I left USF at the end of the year, and began working full-time as a Cab Driver.

As time passed I developed a cordial relationship with two of my white classmates. One of them told me, apologetically, as we had lunch together in the cafeteria that his mother told him to invite some of his friends to their house for holiday cheer, but not any "Negroes". I was uncertain why he wanted to share that conversation with me. He seemed to be a very nice person, genuinely in a dilemma, and may have been looking to me for some guidance or advice on how to reconcile his personal feelings with his mother's admonition. I gave him what help I could by stating that I had made other plans for that date. This was not true, but I thought this might be of some assistance to him. He was embarrassed by this and appeared to be conflicted by the theology he was studying and the practices of his Catholic parents.

The other white student decided to make me the expert on questions about "Negroes." He could not understand why students would sit-in at lunch counters, occupy all the seats and demand to be served when people did not want them there. He regarded such behavior as *"reprehensible"*. It was difficult for him to understand that if one or two African-Americans did this, the probability that they would either be seriously injured or perhaps even killed was substantial. The thing that I found amazing was that he truly seemed to be sincere in asking questions of this nature.

It was obvious that we did not share the same perspective about race relations in the U.S. Hence, I concluded that it would be a waste of my valuable time trying to educate some well-intentioned, but profoundly ignorant white person about what it meant to be an African-American in these United States of America.

When summer arrived, since I was in the naval reserve, I returned to active duty and spent it with the band at the Treasure Island Naval base in the San Francisco Bay. This enabled me to have free room and board as well as a full-time income. My duties consisted essentially of performing in parades and concerts. Although I had been discharged the previous year, I still had two years of reserve time remaining which provided me with the option of spending some of it on active duty.

When summer came to an end, I moved into a room in the *Haight-Ashbury* section of San Francisco near *Golden Gate Park*. It was an aesthetically appealing area and its inhabitants brought back fond memories of France.

When spring arrived, I moved from the room that I had near the university to the Ingleside district of the city. It was a very nice residential neighborhood, with row after row of attractive single-family pastel-colored houses. Nearby were *San Francisco State College* and the City College of San Francisco. I still lived in a room, but it was more attractive with knotty-pine walls and it was located in the basement of a single-family home with a private entrance. The family was exceptionally nice and would often include me in their holiday festivities. Their treatment helped diminish some of my loneliness. I remained there until such time that I was able to afford an apartment.

It has been said that loneliness is a reaction to the absence of significant others; that when lives are without certain significant relationships, we become lonely. Although I had been involved with other women, I would often think of Brigitta and wondered how she was doing. I agonized at the thought of someone else holding her in his arms. My self-esteem had been badly damaged by my experiences at USF, and the future seemed bleak. Yet, I began to acquire a new awareness about myself and American society.

Paul Robeson's autobiography <u>Here I Stand</u> had a profound effect on me. It would enable me to begin to think the unthinkable; no matter who tried to destroy me, I had to be strong enough not to allow it to happen. This society had tried to do it to Robeson, but ultimately, he prevailed.

No one at USF provided me academic advisement or counseling. Supremely confident in my ability, I enrolled in 17 substantive credits my first semester and 11 during the second semester. By the end of the year I had become academically *"disqualified"* to return.

Other Blacks would soon follow. One of the most notable was a young man from the Bahamas who was affectionately nicknamed *Big G*. Eventually, he would go on to graduate from San Francisco State College and subsequently earn law degrees from the University of California at Berkeley and another law degree in England. After that he returned home and became a multi-millionaire and one of the most prominent, if not the most prominent lawyer in the Bahamas.

Ken, my closest friend at USF would graduate but shortly thereafter would go through an incredible metamorphosis. He eventually left the Catholic Church and became a *Yoruba* Priest and Afro centric lecturer and historian. He changed his name to *Baba Adebayo Mamadou Lumumba-Umoja*. Although he came from a strict conservative middle-class Catholic family, he became convinced that fundamental structural changes had to occur in society in order for African-Americans to enjoy their share of the American dream. He would go to Guadalajara, Mexico and then to Washington, D.C., and other places in pursuit of his dream of a society concerned about the health and welfare of all of its people.

My social life at USF had often consisted of frequent chats with the campus barber, Al Hicks, a black man. He was a very congenial and helpful person. He was in his mid-thirties, married with children. He had graduated at the top of his class from USF with a major in Political

Science. He had attended law school at USF for a couple of years but had to discontinue his education due to family responsibilities. He was actively involved in Republican politics and was personally acquainted with former Vice-President Richard Nixon. I would assist him in his unsuccessful, underfinanced campaign for political office. Our relationship developed to such an extent that he would become the best man when I eventually got married.

Confused and uncertain about my future, I got a full-time job driving a Yellow Cab. One evening two young men got in the car and as I listened to their conversation I learned the following: Both were college graduates and in my opinion, neither could chew bubble gum and walk a straight line. In essence, they were dumb. Thus, I concluded that if these two guys could graduate from college as dumb as they were, I knew that I could do likewise.

I enrolled in the City College of San Francisco and remained there for two years. I was thoroughly enjoying the atmosphere and doing satisfactory work and steadily improving each semester from being a "C" student to becoming a "B" student.

My experience at the City College was enough to convince me that I had the intelligence to earn a college degree, and any doubt about that which USF had fostered was removed. The diversity of the student population and the diversity of the professors was a welcome change.

FROM NEGRO TO BECOMING A BLACK MAN

The rise to prominence of Malcolm X in 1958 had a profound effect on me. His ideas and rhetoric caused me to cease using the term "Negro" as a self-referent and to begin using the term Black by 1960. This term meant a state of consciousness and defining one-self rather than having someone else define you. The term African-American was descriptive of the physical person; black was a reference to one's state of mind and being sensitive to ourselves and our interests as a people.

Malcolm embodied our Manhood. He seemed to articulate the most innermost thoughts and feelings of my rapidly expanding peer group. I was more comfortable with his views than those of Dr. King; especially when he spoke about turning the other cheek. Basically, he said if you turn the other cheek, have a fist cocked and be ready to use it against anyone that has hit you. This view was contrary to that which Dr. King espoused. It was not part of my mental makeup to allow someone to physically abuse me and be able to say to them – I still love you. The result of this new feeling of self-pride caused me to seek out and gravitate toward interest groups whose ideology was *"Black Power: By Any Means Necessary."*

As a result of becoming actively involved in groups such as the Oakland/Berkeley based Afro-American Association and the San Francisco *Congress of Racial Equality* (CORE), I would meet and in some instances become acquainted with persons whose names were either well-known or would become well-known in the media. A few such persons were: *Adam Clayton Powell*, the Reverend *Dr. Martin Luther King, Jr., Stokley Carmichael* and his successor, *H. "Rap" Brown*; *Muhammad Ali*, Congressman *Ron Dellums* and Former California Lt. Gov. *Mervin Dymally*; Maya Angelou, *Bobby Seale* and *Huey Newton*, co-founders of the *Black Panther Party* and the incomparable *Maulana Ron Karenga*, to name but a few.

The person with whom I would become friends and who would have tremendous influence on me was a brilliant University of California law student and spellbinding orator – *Donald Warden* a.k.a. *Dr. Haled Abdullah Teri Al-Man* sour He had earned the *Phi Beta Kappa* key at Howard University. He was also a mentor of Black Panther founders, Huey Newton and Bobby Seale. Eventually, he would become an advisor to the Saudi Royal family. He and another doctoral student at Berkeley, Donald Hopkins and fellow law student and future judge and then Dean of the School of Law at Howard University, Henry Ramsey had formed an organization called the Afro-American Association. It attracted some of the brightest and most politically astute and committed African-American men and women in the San Francisco Bay area. It was through this organization that I would begin thinking of myself as an African-American.

Don would often say that our people needed us. We owe our very best, not only to ourselves and our families, but also our communities and we should strive to do nothing less than our very best. He was truly a spell-binding, charismatic speaker.

I acquired insight into the *"ghetto value"* that "Negroes" placed on being a "competent lover" and why we felt we should strive to perfect this art. Additional insight into the short distance "Negroes" had come since slavery and how shackles on the mind had a far greater effect than shackles on one's body was learned. I came to the slow realization that in order to truly become an Afro-American, I had to address attitudes in myself and about myself and my values of beauty, excellence and sacrifice and what was really important in the world that I had never contemplated.

I was taught to strive, not simply for the betterment of myself but my people, and that advancement as a person was inextricably intertwined with the advancement of my people. It was important to know that without a language and culture whose historical antecedents could be traced back to Africa, blacks would become crippled children; helpless against the American conditioning process and the end result invariably would be self-hatred manifested in various ways.

Although raised as a Baptist, I had never learned that the story of Ham in the Bible had been one of the most important factors in the establishment of color prejudice and physical self-hatred among "Negroes". I also learned how the role of the *Christian Church* helped perpetuate among "Negroes" feelings of inferiority, and how the artist Michelangelo, commissioned by Pope Julius II in

1505, created biblical works depicting images of the mother of Jesus and others to resemble Florentine Italians contrary to historical fact.

The Michelangelo paintings influenced the images of the Christ child and the three wise men, the Lord's Supper and the Resurrection to such an extent that eventually there was no evidence of a significant black presence in biblical times contrary to the description of Jesus in Rev. 1:14-15. In essence, Blacks, through white ideology were being brainwashed to worship white images. Standards of beauty were defined by whites in terms that excluded Blacks.

This group of students discussed how Christianity was used by whites who professed to be Christians to enslave blacks; how all progressive aspects of Christianity were either deemphasized or completely eliminated and it was being used to transform the African into "The Negro" through its mass media. Certain standards of beauty were crystallized and these standards simply reinforced the already detrimental process begun by Christianity.

It was argued that the American ideal that put forward *"straight hair as opposed to kinky; straight noses and lips as distinct from flat and broad; and white skin as against black"* for all intent and purpose made the "Negro" helpless because these values were being internalized. We learned that a rhyme that had plagued every black person from childhood to death was: *"If you're white, you're alright; if you're brown, stick around, but if you're black, stay back."*

We also learned that in the area of education that the basic school problem for African-Americans was one of providing initiative, and not legal desegregation In essence, the right to go to school, but not having the desire to learn is meaningless. What was stressed was how important it was for African-Americans to take the initiative to study, not for themselves per se, but for their people because their people needed them.

The good intentions of the various civil rights organizations were acknowledged, however, but were deficient in some significant way. Northern whites received Dr. King as the black *Gandhi* of America. King's famous remark: "We will wear them out with suffering even if we are killed" had been proclaimed from California to Maine. It was the view of many of us that Dr. King had not angered many Northern whites because in some respect he did not require that whites consider the "Negro" as a human being.

Virtually all of us in attendance, especially those of us from the North thought it was personally repugnant to even entertain the thought of permitting some demented white person to spit on us and subject us to all sorts of personal abuse and degradation without seeking to send such a person to meet his maker. It was Malcolm X and not Dr. King who had the greatest appeal to many of us.

We learned that after this socialization process, the extent to which a black person could boast of pride and dignity related directly to the degree to which the white social, religious and political structure recognized him as a full man. And without his language and culture and without respect for his heritage, the "Negro" became a crippled child; he was helpless against the American conditioning process, and after more than two centuries of enslavement, the white man employed every means to stamp a feeling of natural inferiority into the soul of the "Negro."

I had never been in a small intimate group where anyone had such eloquent and fiery rhetoric. It was argued that the mind-set of whites, stated or unstated was reflected in the Dred Scott U.S. Supreme Court decision, Chief Justice Taney said:

"A Negro has no rights which a white man need respect."

The gist of this argument was that emancipated or not "Negroes" remained subject to the authority of whites and had no right or privilege but such as those who held the power and government might choose to grant them.

It was through the Afro-American Association that I would meet the woman I would marry after knowing her for less than a month. Physically, she was an attractive, sinuous looking brown-skinned woman with her hair in a natural coiffure. When she spoke, her English was flawless and her voice had a sultry resonant quality. Her questions or comments revealed a first-class mind. When the meeting was over, I introduced myself to her. The next meeting of the group was scheduled to be at my apartment in San Francisco. Her name was *Martha,* but she preferred to be called *Marti*. I extended her a special invitation to attend. She understood the double message I conveyed.

At our next meeting, Marti was one of the first person's to arrive. We agreed to have dinner together the following weekend. She indicated that I could drive her home in her car and keep the car for my personal use until we got together again. To say that I was impressed would be a mild understatement. We were unable to keep our date because she had to be hospitalized for a minor problem. I visited her regularly and brought her home from the hospital. Within a few weeks after our meeting, we were married in 1962.

During the time I lived in San Francisco, I had become a very lonely person notwithstanding the fact that I dated and partied frequently. Female companionship was not the problem it had been at the University of San Francisco. Before I got married, my roommates and I often had parties on weekend that were well attended by young ladies of all hues from around the bay area, yet, there was a void in my life that dates and casual sexual encounters no longer satisfied. I had a need to feel that I belonged to someone; a need to create my own family.

My marriage to Martha would last 22 years and our first and only child, consistent with the mood of the times would be named after the Haitian revolutionary – *Toussaint L'Ouverture*. I was impressed by the fact that Toussaint, a former slave, had become a revolutionary and brilliant military commander. He organized the slaves of Haiti to defeat over 50,000 of Napoleon's crack troops that had been sent to Haiti to quash the freedom movement that had started there.

Although it was not taught in any school that I attended, the Louisiana Purchase, one of the largest land purchases made by this country in its history, was due in large measure to Francois Dominique Toussaint L'Ouverture. He had halted Napoleon's expansionist plans and created the opportunity for the United States to expand.

Sometimes I Feel Like a Fatherless Child

SAN FRANCISCO – AND THE STRUGGLE TO BE

When I married Martha in 1962 she had already graduated from San Francisco State College but worked in the Registrar's office at the college. After reviewing my work at the community college she encouraged me to apply for admission to San Francisco State because the City College could not do anything else for me. I did this and was admitted shortly thereafter. She was a tremendous source of support emotionally and otherwise for me for 22 years. I loved her very much—yet—my background as an only child with no mother or father as role models did not make me a very good marriage mate. Periodically, she would say that she would give me a grade of "A" as a Father but a grade of "C" as a husband.

One of the things that I learned about the city of San Francisco in a short period of time was that it was a city that had a disproportionate number of well- educated persons working in positions that some might regard as menial, especially when one considered their level of education. There were those with Master's or Doctoral degrees working as clerks, meter-men, meter-maids or Janitors. The reasons appeared quite similar. They were striving to be artists, writers or actors. They were working simply to provide themselves with the basic necessities so that their energies could be devoted to producing the next great Novel or Play that would be made into a movie or some other major artistic undertaking.

Noel Myricks

San Francisco had a cable car driver writing plays and novels which would become films and in which he would perform and direct *(Melvin Van Peebles)*; it was a meeting at a CORE function and conversing with a lovely, charming and indescribably eloquent African-American woman such as Maya Angelou. San Francisco was working with a young Rehabilitation Counselor out of Penn State University who sang at local clubs in the evening who reminded me of a young male imitation of Ella Fitzgerald (*Al Jarreau*). San Francisco was a bright, ambitious young African-American out of Texas who had graduated from San Francisco State and enrolled in Hastings, the University of California School of Law in San Francisco (*Willie Brown*); a person who would go on to become one of the most influential persons in California politics and who eventually became the Mayor of San Francisco.

When I sought Willie out for advice after acquiring a Master's degree as to whether I should go to law school or move to Los Angeles to become part of *Merv Dymally's* political machine, he offered it without hesitation.

He said, "Noel, if you go to L.A., when Merv says jump, your only option will be – how high? If you go and get your law degree, you do not have to answer to anyone. If someone tells you to do something that you do not want to do, you can tell them to kiss your [expletive]."

I followed his advice and have never regretted it.

Sometimes I Feel Like a Fatherless Child

San Francisco would be my exposure to those persons described in the media as *Beatniks, Hippies* and *Flower Children*. It would be my first exposure to the Irish and Italian political machines as a result of working in the campaigns of *Phil* and *John Burton*. I would learn from Phil Burton the meaning of the political axiom: *"Never get mad; get even."*

The people of San Francisco were as diverse and multifaceted as the geography of the city itself. How do you describe for a person who has never done it, what it is like to drive across the Golden Gate Bridge when the Sun is setting and the fog is settling in? How does one describe a man known by many as *A Lion in Court – Vincent Hallinan*? Or *The King of Torts – Melvin Belli* and the incomparable *Jake Ehrlich*, whose book *"Never Plead Guilty"* has been on my bookshelf for years.

There are no words that could adequately describe San Francisco's Poet *Laureate* of the Beat era of the fifties and the owner of the *City Lights Bookstore, Lawrence Ferlinghetti*. This was the place where artists and writers would gather for poetry readings and philosophical discussions about the issues confronting mankind. The Reverend *Cecil Williams* and the *Glide Memorial Church* was a place regarded by many as a place of profound spiritual renewal, with its ecumenical congregation and view of the world. San Francisco was the place to be in the sixties, and it was home for me.

San Francisco was not without its problems. It was cool initially to the arrival of Willie Mays whom many

Italians perceived as a threat to the esteem of their hometown hero, *Joe DiMaggio*. Nonetheless, the people eventually accepted the *Say Hey Kid* after the Giants came to San Francisco in 1960.

My job as a Yellow Cab driver was a thoroughly enjoyable experience, especially the tips. It offered me an opportunity to have access to an automobile and the freedom to patrol the entire city.

Periodically, I would review the job ads for other opportunities and often found myself taking examinations for employment with the city, state or federal government. They ranged from those of Janitor, Postal Clerk, Correctional Officer at San Quentin and Deputy Sheriff for the City and County of San Francisco. More often than not I successfully passed these examinations and periodically would rotate between various jobs while trying to stay focused on the direction my life should take.

While I enjoyed being a Yellow Cab driver, eventually I had to leave it. One evening I stopped to pick up a white male at the Greyhound Bus Station. Although he appeared to be in his early thirties, he projected a *"Joe College"* image, and in the minds of some cab drivers appeared to be a *safe* pickup.

When he got in the cab he sat directly behind me. I felt some mild discomfort at this because most people would sit behind the front passenger seat. Nonetheless, I shrugged it off because of his safe appearance.

When I asked where he wanted to go he said, "Twin Peaks."

That made me feel good.

Twin Peaks is at the top of Market Street, the main street in downtown San Francisco, and it was one of the more scenic areas in the city. It was a fairly typical December night for San Francisco. The fog was somewhat heavier than usual but this seemed to add to the mystique of the city, especially with Christmas ornaments seemingly everywhere.

When we arrived near the top of Twin Peaks, I asked the passenger to give me more specific directions. Eventually, he led me to a dead-end street.

I heard him whisper, "Okay Driver. Give me your money."

His voice was so low that I thought I might be hallucinating; perhaps unduly influenced by the mystic quality of the night. I immediately switched on the light inside the cab and turned to collect my fare. To my utter shock I found myself looking directly in the barrel of a large blue revolver.

What was particularly unsettling was the fact that the guy's hand, the one with the gun in it was shaking just inches from my face. I thought the gun might go off at any second.

In a commanding voice he said, "Cut off the light; cut off the light and put your hands down."

When I saw the gun I immediately whirled around and faced the front and put my hands in the air and then complied with his request.

After a long pause which enabled me to regain some of my composure, I decided to try to get him to relax so that I would not be killed. I had no intention whatsoever of being shot for the approximately forty dollars in my pocket that belonged to Yellow Cab.

When he demanded the money again, I retorted: "Look my man, point that gun toward the floor. Neither of us needs an accident to happen because of forty or fifty dollars. Just cool it; you can have all of Yellow Cab's money, just point that gun toward the floor and be cool."

I announced that I was going to go in my pocket and come out with a lump of bills, and if he saw me tugging at my pocket, not to get nervous because I did not have a weapon on me.

He said, "I know you cab drivers don't carry guns."

I pulled the money out of my pocket and gave it to him.

Then, to my surprise, he said: "Take off your hat and give it to me, and leave the keys in the car, and slowly, get out of the car."

Both of us got out of the cab simultaneously.

By this time I had regained my composure and thought, for a fleeting moment as the robber was standing next to me, that I might be able to hit him with a karate chop across his Adams apple as he moved toward the driver's seat. He seemed to have read my mind.

He said, "Don't try anything or I'll kill you."

I quickly dismissed whatever thoughts I had of trying to be a hero. He got in the cab and drove off. I went to a nearby house and got a resident to call the police.

After reporting this incident to the police, who took me to the Yellow Cab station, I filed a report and went home. I tried to drive again the following day but I found myself becoming too nervous every time someone sat behind me. Shortly thereafter, I received an offer from the City and County of San Francisco to work temporarily as a Deputy Sheriff. This came about as a result of an examination I had taken and successfully passed earlier in the year. I left Yellow Cab permanently.

The job of the Deputy Sheriff in San Francisco was essentially that of a jailer. You patrolled the cell blocks where people were incarcerated. While patrolling the cell block one day, I noticed a familiar face. Ironically, it was the guy that had robbed me. I couldn't believe it. I walked up to the cell for a closer look. It was the same guy who had robbed me a few weeks earlier. He had not recognized me. I suspect it was because my image as a Deputy Sheriff was quite different from my image as a Yellow Cab driver.

He had been apprehended robbing a drug store approximately a week earlier and was being held in jail until his trial. After this experience, I suspect that both of us had a greater appreciation for the statement that *"Fate works in a strange way."*

A Period of Rapid Growth and Change

When my temporary appointment expired after the holidays, my name came up for a temporary position as a Correctional Officer at the San Quentin Penitentiary—I seized that opportunity. I knew that San Quentin was the oldest prison in California and all male inmates who were condemned to die were housed there.

Within a day or so after my arrival I was informed by an older officer that they were going to "break me in right." What he meant by this was that I was going to witness an execution. I had mixed emotions but concealed them. I had observed executions in the movies and wondered how they would compare to the real thing. I would find out soon enough.

A couple of days later I found myself along with other witnesses standing around an enclosed area in the basement. It was the gas chamber. It separated us from the inmate, who appeared to be a *Hispanic* male. We stood behind a thick glass. It resembled a large green box that was approximately six feet across, eight feet high with a chimney to exhale the gas.

The inmate was escorted from a holding cell accompanied by a priest and two correctional officers into the gas chamber. There were two chairs, with straps and a container underneath the seat of each chair. As he entered, he appeared to look directly in my eyes and I felt uncomfortable. He was dressed in blue jeans, the kind sailors wear while working at sea. He also had on a clean white shirt and he walked with soft sandals. His eyes appeared somewhat glassy, as though he was under the influence of alcohol or drugs. It was also a rather common expression among boxers who had been stunned by a punch and were ready to be put away. I lowered my head; momentarily embarrassed, somewhat ashamed at the absence of privacy for this man whom society, through its instrumentality of the Court, had decided should pay with his life for what he had done.

His arms and chest were strapped into the chair and a stethoscope was placed on his chest where his heart was located. One of the correctional officers patted him twice on his shoulder as if to say goodbye. There was no response from the inmate.

The air-tight pressurized chamber was sealed, and pellets of sodium cyanide, the size of eggs were dropped into the container underneath which had a mixture of sulfuric acid under the seat. After a few moments, the inmate suddenly became profuse with sweat and struggled to get air as he choked; his body jerking back and forth and his face began to turn red. Eventually, his body relaxed and he slumped forward. There was a brief period of silence and then the Warden announced the time that the prisoner's heart had stopped beating, and then he stated that the execution was completed and we were excused.

As I walked to the witness room and prepared to sign the witness book, a visual picture of his horrendous deed quickly flashed through my mind. He had robbed a store in San Jose, California and unbeknownst to him, a silent alarm had gone off. When he exited the store, a lone policeman was waiting for him and blocked his vehicle. They began shooting at each other. The policeman was wounded and fell to the ground and the guy walked over and emptied his gun in the head of the policeman. The policeman was married with children.

By the time this temporary appointment came to an end, my name had come up for a permanent part-time job with the U.S. Post Office. It was an ideal job because it would enable me to earn enough money to afford an apartment and attend to my basic necessities while attending college.

While working at the post office I met an ex-Navy man, Cordell Boyd. We got along well and decided to rent an apartment together. We found one in the Ingleside district near my friend from USF, Al Hicks. This arrangement worked well until Cordell got married and moved to Los Angeles where he eventually became a Hollywood Camera man.

I subsequently met a native San Franciscan at the post office who, coincidentally, had the same name as my boyhood friend, Charles Anderson. He was residing at the family home in the Richmond district. He wanted to move out and share an apartment with someone. He was also pursuing studies at the City College of San Francisco. We became roommates and were eventually joined by another student, *Octavious Tracy.*

The three of us remained roommates until I got married and moved into another apartment with my wife. Often we studied, socialized and partied together and even had some of the same classes. We thoroughly enjoyed engaging each other in philosophical arguments into the wee hours of the morning as we promoted each other's mutual growth and development. None of us at that point in time had any idea that the three of us would eventually acquire doctoral degrees in our chosen fields and achieve some measure of success in our respective professions.

Charles would earn a Ph.D., in Economics from Stanford; Tracy would earn a Ph.D., in Psychology from the University of California at San Francisco and I would earn a J.D., in law from Howard University and an Ed.D. in Higher Education from the American University in Washington, D.C.

We had some memorable experiences as roommates. With the Vietnam War increasing in its level of intensity—Tracy received a notice that he had been drafted. To say that he found this to be disconcerting would be an understatement. He would often state that his priority was his education, not fighting someone whom he did not know in some place called Vietnam. He concocted every conceivable scheme imaginable to avoid the draft but none worked. Finally, he was paid a visit by a couple of white F.B.I. agents.

They had a cordial discussion and even chatted about some of the Black Power literature on our book shelf. The meeting concluded with the agents informing Tracy that they had enjoyed meeting and talking to him, but if he did not show up on the date he was scheduled to appear to be inducted into the Army, their next meeting would not be so cordial. Tracy got the message loud and clear. Begrudgingly, he made his appearance and served his time honorably.

There was an occasion where I had neglected to pay some traffic tickets. One day as I casually glanced out of my apartment window, I saw two policemen get out of their car and proceed toward our apartment. Intuitively, I knew they were coming for me due to my failure to pay the parking tickets. I quickly went into the closet, climbed a ladder to the roof, and proceeded to leap from building to building to escape. Shortly thereafter, I went and paid the traffic tickets to avoid any future problems with the police.

San Francisco State

The University of California at Berkeley and its surrounding atmosphere had always been in the vanguard of campus movements. Discussions in the restaurants and coffee klatches provided an education itself. The Free Speech Movement which would sweep the country would be spearheaded by a Berkeley student, *Mario Savio*.

San Francisco State was a microcosm of UC Berkeley. The atmosphere at San Francisco State and the city of San Francisco was an exciting place to be in the sixties. My time at San Francisco State was a period of considerable growth and development. I thoroughly enjoyed the atmosphere and the diversity of both the student population and the professors. Initially, I participated in Air Force ROTC, with the thought of earning a degree and returning to active duty as an Air Force officer. I lived on campus in married student housing, and was elected President of the Married Student Housing Association.

By 1965 I had earned a bachelor's degree in Psychology and had been accepted to do graduate work, with scholarships at various institutions, including the University of California at Berkeley, Michigan State University and at San Francisco State. I had also successfully passed the Air Force Officer's Qualifying Examination and was offered a commission as an Air Force Officer.

I wanted to be commissioned but I also wanted the Master's degree. However, I was informed that if I accepted the commission, I would have to go on active duty immediately and would not receive a deferment to complete the Master's. Furthermore, it appeared that the government was increasing the number of military personnel being sent to Vietnam, and I surmised that the probability was quite high that I would have to leave my family for service there, and I was not prepared to do that. Based on this analysis, I decided to remain at San Francisco State to pursue the Master's degree in Rehabilitation Counseling.

This would mean that I would be able to remain in Married Student Housing and have a two-year scholarship which would take care of most of my financial needs. I proceeded through the two year Master's program with relative ease and acquired it in 1967. My undergraduate work in Psychology had prepared me extremely well for this endeavor.

My wife and I flew my aunt Mary Lou out so that she could be present when I received the Master's degree. This was her first time on an airplane. We subsequently had dinner at a four star restaurant in Sausalito in Marin County across the Golden Gate bridge. She asked to see the bill when it came and her response was: "Whoopee! Baby Junior, I could buy groceries for a week with this." I smiled and realized, perhaps for the first time how far I had come since my childhood, and the lifestyle to which I had become accustomed.

Married Student Housing at San Francisco State consisted of 60 two bedroom apartments, with a total cost which included utilities of forty-five dollars ($45.00) per month. The facilities were the old World War II temporary housing. They were clean and reasonably well-kept.

Nonetheless, while pursuing the Master's degree, the College Administration decided to take action to close these facilities so that the construction of newer and more costly apartments could be developed. Those of us in Married Student housing opposed this and we met to decide what course of action to pursue. It was decided that each family would contribute fifty Dollars ($50.00) and we would seek legal representation to protect our interests.

A controversy arose over who we would select as our attorney. One of the residents had a friend who was an attorney who offered his services at minimal cost. My analysis of the situation was that we needed legal representation, but we needed more than an ordinary attorney because our effort was really a public relations effort. I pointed out that a comparative analysis of the power positions of the college administration with those of us in married student housing mandated it. It was stressed that we had two battles to win: one was the public relations battle and the other was a possible legal battle.

Based on this analysis, I proposed that we seek to retain the services of the "King of Torts" - Melvin Belli. It was pointed out that his appearance on our behalf would generate considerable publicity in the media which would accrue to our benefit, and it was this sort of publicity that we would get which we would not otherwise be able to afford. The question was put to a vote and my position won by a landslide.

Two of the other officers and I went to Melvin Belli's office. We were impressed the moment we entered. He had enlarged copies of checks from cases he had won and news articles of substantial judgments framed and on his wall. The man himself was quite impressive. He seemed amused at the amount of money we had to retain him, yet, he was interested enough in our plight to take the case. He perceived his effort on our behalf as pro bono work. When we returned to the campus we felt as though we were floating on a cloud.

Gatorville was the name given to the Married Student Housing complex. We quickly prepared a press release for the local media and the campus newspaper. The campus newspaper quickly came out with its paper and in big, bold print on its front page, the headlines read, *"Belli to Represent Gatorville."*

The administration read this and there were immediate inquiries as to whether or not it was true. When it was confirmed we received veiled threats which we ignored. Melvin Belli arrived on campus in his *Rolls-Royce* with one of his associates. I, along with the two other officers met him and accompanied him to the office of the President. It was exciting to be privy to their negotiations and to observe skills that I would find useful when I became a lawyer.

When we entered the office of the President to meet with him and a member of his staff, I could detect tension on their part. Instead of creating an adversarial situation immediately, Melvin Belli was charming. He began telling humorous stories that seemed to have no relationship to why we were there. Eventually, I concluded that this was a tactic to reduce the tension and put everyone at ease.

When it appeared that the tension had subsided, Belli stated that he was certain that we could find some common ground which would enable those of us who were married students to remain in the Married Student Housing complex and complete our education, and at the same time address any concerns that the administration had about our safety.

The President's stated position was that the facilities were old and the electrical wiring was defective, and the university was not prepared to assume the risk of injury or worse to the students, hence, we had to move. Belli raised questions about the basis for concluding that the electrical wiring problems required eviction rather than minor repairs. He pointed out that based on his experience in dealing with matters of this nature as a member of the State Fire Board, he was confident that constructive action could be taken to address the concerns raised by the President that would not have to necessitate our eviction.

Belli then proposed a course of action that would meet the stated concerns of all the parties. He recited, by memory, certain key provisions of the State Fire Code to politely correct any misstatement made by a university official. As I watched this process, I simply found myself in awe of Belli. It was as though I was watching an artist paint a masterpiece. When the college administration could no longer defend its position on the grounds that they had articulated the meeting was adjourned.

Within a short time after this meeting the dispute was settled. We had prevailed and the university agreed to incur the costs to make the necessary repairs to our facilities.

It was party-time in Gatorville! Other officers and I rode around our community with horns blaring, waving to the other residents who were elated at the news. Parties lasted until the wee hours of the morning.

There had been a feeling, albeit unsubstantiated, that university officials, through some politicians were being pressured to build new dormitories where the prices charged would be more in line with what apartments in the area would cost. This would have been a great opportunity for real estate developers to make money. Our attitude was simple and direct – Not at our expense. Shortly thereafter, the President of the College resigned and returned to the East Coast University from whence he had come.

Sometimes I Feel Like a Fatherless Child

Departing the City by the Bay

As I approached the completion of the Master's program in 1967, I applied to some law schools and Ph.D., programs and was accepted at every place where I had applied. Based on what was occurring in the United States, and my experiences in the bay area, I had a keen interest in Civil Rights. I had arrived in San Francisco as a bright-eyed, enthusiastic "Negro", and I was leaving as a more mature and informed African-American with a well-developed ideology and I wanted to commit myself to making a contribution to the progress of my people. I had the good fortune of being exposed to some people whose ideas would bring about change in America and the way many Americans, especially African-Americans viewed themselves.

It had been a turbulent period. It was during this period that Mack Charles Parker was taken from jail and lynched in Mississippi. Herbert Lee, a voter-registration worker had been killed by a white legislator in Liberty, Mississippi. The Freedom Rides had begun in 1961, and within days a bus had been bombed and burned in Alabama. 1962 saw 12,000 federal marshals escorting *James Meredith* to classes at the *University of Mississippi. Roman Duckworth* would be killed by police in Mississippi after being taken off a bus. In Alabama, William Lewis Moore would be slain in 1963 during his one-man march against segregation there. Four little school girls would be killed in a bombing of the 16th Street Baptist Church in

Birmingham. *Medgar Evers*, the Field Secretary of the NAACP in Mississippi would be assassinated in front of his home in Jackson, Mississippi.

An estimated 250,000 people would stage the largest Civil Rights demonstration in recent history. While sitting in a creative writing course at the City College of San Francisco, an announcement would come over the public address system that President John Fitzgerald Kennedy had been assassinated in Dallas, Texas.

Although I did not know it at the time, 1963 would be the last time that I would see *El Hajj Malik El Shabazz* aka Malcolm X alive. I had met him at the Muslim Mosque in San Francisco prior to his presentation at the University of California in Berkeley in October 1963. I would always remember his words:

"We believe in a fair exchange: An eye for an eye; a tooth for a tooth; a head for a head and a life for a life. If this is the price of freedom, we won't hesitate to pay the price."

I beamed with pride and the adrenalin flowed upon hearing these words.

1964 saw the murder of *James Chaney, Andrew Goodman* and *Michael Schwerner*, three civil rights workers who were slain near Philadelphia, Mississippi in Nashoba County. Andrew Goodman and Michael Schwerner had gone there from New York, like so many other whites of good will to work in voter registration rallies for CORE. They had investigated the burning of Mt. Zion Methodist

Church, which had served as a site for the CORE Freedom School. They were arrested and subsequently freed and then subsequently stopped shortly after their release by the Klan and murdered.

The Reverend *James Reeb* and Mrs. *Viola Liuzzo* from Detroit would be killed in Alabama while trying to bring about constructive social change in these United States of America. Malcolm X would be assassinated on February 21, 1965 and eventually, on April 4, 1968, I would learn while driving home from law school, that Martin Luther King, Jr., had been assassinated.

Finally, Congress, under the leadership of Congressman Adam Clayton Powell and President Johnson would finally act and pass the first and most significant piece of civil rights legislation of the era – the 1964 Civil Rights Act.

The body count of Americans dying in Vietnam was increasing. By the end of December 1966, 385,000 U.S. troops were serving in Vietnam and paying a terrible price. The Vietnam Memorial which was eventually erected for American dead has served as a living testimony to the lives that were simply wasted for no legitimate reason.

The United States was engaged in two wars – one was abroad in Vietnam and the other, which was the more important one, was here at home. Vital resources that could have been used in the War on Poverty and brought relief to so many people in need of assistance were being wasted in Vietnam.

This country was confronted with what I and many others regarded as the most important moral issue of the last half of the 20th century – the future of race relations in the United States. Churches were being burned; homes were being bombed and too many murderers were being freed by white juries for this country to hold itself out to the world as a role-model of freedom worthy of emulation. I had learned during the course of my education that an idea was something that could not be destroyed with a bullet; it had to be defeated by a more attractive idea. And that idea was making the American way of life more attractive than other alternatives. I became resolved to prepare myself to the fullest extent possible to make my contribution, however small, to bring about constructive social change in our society.

While working in the campaign of Congressman Phil Burton in 1966, I met Phil Ryan, a brilliant young white law student enrolled at Howard University. I was intrigued by his political savoir-faire and the comments he made about his experiences at Howard. His involvement in the case of _Powell v. McCormick_ was particularly interesting. Phil was the research assistant to Professor _Herbert O. Reid,_ one of Adam Clayton Powell's co-counsels. He stated that not only was he doing research on the case, but that one of the major advantages of attending Howard was that a student would be able to be present at the U.S. Supreme Court to see how his research material was used in oral arguments.

He added that the University of California at Berkeley, which I was also considering, would not afford me that sort of opportunity. When I challenged him by asking whether he was suggesting that the library at Howard could compete with the library at Berkeley, he said "No." And then he added, "But the Library of Congress, which you have easy access to can certainly compete and compete quite well with the library at UC Berkeley."

Adam Clayton Powell had been a boyhood idol. I had met him briefly when he spoke at the Third Baptist Church in San Francisco. I admired him because of his brilliance and apparent ability to be a free-spirited African-American who seemed to be able to do whatever he wanted to do with relative impunity. Yet, there was also a very serious side to this man. He was, for all intent and purpose, and had been for a very long time, the person in the U.S. Congress whom African Americans all over the country looked to for assistance at the national level. By the time he would leave the Congress, he would see over 60 pieces of major social domestic legislation sponsored by him signed into law by President Lyndon Baines Johnson.

The War on Poverty would be the cornerstone of his social legislation. There was legislation for Aid to Handicapped Children and Child Safety; Urban Fellowships; Summer Jobs for Youth and the Elementary and Secondary School Act. All Americans would benefit from Powell's work and sheer brilliance. Notwithstanding this, there would be those in the Congress who could not tolerate him and would seek to destroy him. In my opinion, this was what <u>Powell v. McCormick</u> was all about and the people at Howard, as had been the case historically, were at the vanguard of civil rights litigation.

One late spring day in 1967 I came home and turned on the television. There was a new story about students at Howard University demonstrating. The cameras focused on one young law student – *Jay Green*. He was impeccably attired and an eloquent speaker. He reminded me of a young Malcolm X. I sat on the couch and listened attentively to him. He was speaking to a large number of student demonstrators and describing some members of the campus administration as "Handkerchief head Uncle Tom's" who were no longer relevant to the movement. He went on to talk about the need for new leadership for the challenges that Black Americans faced today. When the news story ended, I turned to my wife and informed her that I had decided to attend the School of Law at Howard in the Fall.

Sometimes I Feel Like a Fatherless Child

COLLEGE EXPERIENCE

Howard University

My family and I came to Washington, D.C. in August 1967, approximately one week before the start of my law classes. We checked into the Ramada Inn and the following day contacted friends from the Afro-American Association who had come to Washington from Berkley. They had indicated that when we got to Washington they would assist us in locating an apartment. Within a matter of a few hours we found an apartment which was located on Georgia Avenue, in the upper northwest section of Washington. It was very convenient because it would enable me to travel by bus directly to the law school which was approximately 15 minutes away.

After spending the next few days settling into the apartment, I visited the law school for the first time. As I walked the halls, I found myself somewhat puzzled by the fact that all of the pictures hanging on the walls were pictures of white persons.

When I walked into the student lounge to meet some of the students who were there, the student whom I saw on television, Jay Green was among them. He was surrounded by a small group of students and they were engaged in an animated discussion. As I listened to it, I was shocked to learn that Jay had been dismissed from Howard albeit he was an honor student. He had fallen into disfavor with university officials, ostensibly because of his student protest activities.

Noel Myricks

He did not take his dismissal passively. He had filed a lawsuit captioned, <u>Greene v. Howard University,</u> with the assistance of some of his law professors. I had looked forward to getting to know him, and now I would be denied this opportunity. Jay was young, gifted and an African-American. He lost his case in the lower court but a division of an appeals court ordered the university to allow him to reenroll to complete the semester. After that he applied to the law school at Yale where he was accepted. He would go on to earn the *Juris Doctoris* in Law and a Master's degree in Economics. It did not take too long for me to realize that that this was not San Francisco State or the University of California at Berkley where there was considerable tolerance for Free Speech.

Shortly at the end of my first civil procedure class I asked my Civil Procedure professor, *Elwood "Chick" Chisolm* why there were no pictures on the walls of African-Americans such as *Paul Robeson, W.E.B. DuBois* and others.

He looked at me in a rather condescending manner and said in a slow South Carolina drawl, "Mr. Myricks, here at Howard Law we only hang pictures on the wall of prominent lawyers or judges, and since Mr. Robeson was not a lawyer or judge, it would not be appropriate to have his picture on the wall."

I smiled and said, "With all due respect Professor, it's obvious that you do not know your Black History well, because if you did, you would know that after graduating from Rutgers University, Paul Robeson attended

Columbia University School of Law where he was a classmate of Mr. Justice Douglas. He graduated from there with honors and he subsequently practiced law on Wall Street. His briefs were used to win several cases for very big corporate clients and he asked a Senior Partner when he would be given the opportunity to represent these clients in court and he was denied it.

Robeson overheard some of the attorneys in the locker room laughing at the fact that he thought he would actually be given the opportunity to go to court and represent these corporate clients. After this incident, he left the firm and the profession of law and went into the theatre." I continued by stating that if he'd like I could provide him with documentation to support what I had said.

He glared at me and said, "Do that!"

One of the students who had been privy to this conversation tapped me on the arm discreetly and nodded for me to follow him out of the class. As we exited he asked where I had gone to undergraduate college. When I said San Francisco State, he looked at me and said, "Homeboy, my name is *Elton Long*. I'm from Sacramento, California. You don't know it but you have just flunked this class."

I was taken aback by his comment, and when I inquired as to what he meant, he said, "This is not San Francisco State where you can say what you want to your professors; this is HOWARD. I attended undergraduate school here, and it is quite different from what you experienced in the California State College System. You do not talk back to these people here or make them look stupid. If they want to get you, they will; you saw what happened to *Jay Green*, and he was an honor student. This is your first year."

He laughed and continued, "All those notions you have about freedom of speech and academic freedom; forget them until you get back to California. If you don't watch yourself, you'll be going back sooner than you had expected. 'Chick' is one of the most influential professors in this School."

After this incident, Elton and I became inseparable friends as he served as a guide for me through the social and cultural milieu that was the law school at Howard. His brother had graduated from the law school a year previously and had briefed him on what to do and what not to do in the law school as well as the idiosyncrasies of the different professors and the politics of the school.

Elton and other students familiar with the culture of the School told me to my disbelief that no matter what I wrote, I would not pass Civil Procedure. However, Elton came up with a strategy that I should use to avoid this outcome.

Based on my psychology background, I had become the student assistant to Professor *Paul Diggs* and assisted him in his test construction methods program. Professor Diggs and Professor Chisolm were good friends. Elton suggested that shortly before the time that I was scheduled to take the final examination in Civil Procedure, I should get ill and use that as an excuse not to take it. Elton surmised that if I could buy some time, Professor Diggs could intervene on my behalf and defuse some of the animosity Professor Chisolm had toward me.

Based on the rules of the law school, if I became ill and was unable to take the exam when scheduled, I could do so at another time. At the appropriate time I did this. Professor Chisolm angrily allowed me to take the exam at another time.

Professor Diggs agreed to intervene on my behalf and also advised me to wait until the fall to take the examination because by that time "Chick" would have "cooled off." I followed his advice.

After talking to Professor Chisolm, Professor Diggs told me that "Chick", the name he used for Professor Chisolm got angry with me because of what he perceived as an arrogant attitude on my part. He added, although Professor Chisolm may not have known that Paul Robeson was a lawyer, it was presumptuous of me to tell him that he did not know his Black History. He stated that as a South Carolinian, Professor Chisolm had lived through some of the worse aspects of Black History while I sat on my rear-end in the navy and places like San Francisco and read about it.

He related the following story that occurred during the fifties with Professor Chisolm. He said that 'Chick" had been sent by the NAACP to Alabama to defend a

Black client before a racist judge and jury. While Professor Chisolm was advocating for his client, the judge turned his back to Professor Chisolm and would not accord him the dignity and respect to which he was entitled. Eventually, when this insulting behavior by the Judge exceeded Professor Chisolm's level of tolerance he blurted out, "You bald-headed [expletive], turn around here and give me the respect you give other lawyers."

The judge turned around, with a face as red as a tomato, and yelled to the bailiff, "Take this Nigger away and lock him up."

Professor Diggs went on to point out that this was simply one of several clashes that Professor Chisolm had with *"southern justice"* as he advocated in a hostile environment for Blacks.

Professor Diggs concluded by describing the legal team which developed the strategy for <u>Brown v. Board of Education.</u> He pointed out that although Thurgood Marshall got most of the publicity surrounding the Brown decision because he was the chief advocate, Marshall had some of the best legal minds in the country supporting him and one of his key strategists was Elwood "Chick" Chisolm. When I returned in the fall, I took the Civil Procedure examination and received a final grade of 70 and I did not complain or bother Professor Chisolm again.

I had looked forward to my class in Torts. The professor scheduled to teach the course was Patricia Roberts Harris, who at that time was preparing to leave her position as Ambassador to the United Nations. She had a reputation as a brilliant law professor. However when classes began, it was discovered that her husband, an Administrative Law Judge in the Federal government would be substituting for her until she could leave the UN. Torts was scheduled to be a year in length and there was only one examination. We learned when the class began that Mr. Harris would be responsible for the class for one semester until his wife could complete her duties as an Ambassador.

Although most students were disappointed, no one was expressing their disappointment publicly. After several very boring classes with Mr. Harris, who seemed totally unprepared, he began a class by reading a law journal article to us for approximately 35 to 40 minutes. Students seemed bored and inattentive. He occasionally glanced up at students. Finally, I raised my hand in disgust. It was held up without him acknowledging it for quite a while. Students would snicker at the fact that he had not noticed it, but no one would speak up.

Finally, when he saw me, he squinted and with an expression on his face as though raising my hand was a source of irritation he said, "Yes? Do you have a question?"

I stood up and said, "Mr. Harris, with all due respect, I traveled 3,000 miles to study law here at Howard. If the article that you are reading is so important that you would consume three-quarters of our class time reading it to us, why didn't you have it duplicated and put on reserve in the library and make it assigned reading? You have wasted our time sir. You should give every student in this class the benefit of being literate until there is evidence to the contrary. This entire class session has been a waste of time for many of us." He was a fair-complexioned black man who turned livid.

A student sitting on the left side of me leaped to his feet and quickly moved over several seats and began yelling to the professor, "This man doesn't speak for me; he doesn't speak for me."

At that point the rest of the class broke out in laughter. When the laughter subsided, Professor Harris looked at me with tight lips and piercing eyes and said, "What is your name?"

I said, "Myricks, that's M.Y.R.I.C.K.S. Noel Myricks." After I said that, he slammed the book on the desk and walked out of class.

Afterwards, several students came to me and congratulated me for doing what I had done, and admitted that they wanted to do something to that effect but did not have the nerve to do so. Some verbally chastised the student who said that I did not speak for him. He flunked out at the end of the year.

When the class commenced again, Professor Harris immediately singled me out and asked me to give a case that had not been assigned. This was a weak effort to humiliate me. I told him that I did not have that case because it had not been assigned but if he wanted me to do one of the assigned cases, I would be glad to do so. He left me alone after that response.

When the end of the first semester came to an end, Patricia Roberts Harris replaced her husband. Once again, Elton long advised me that if I passed her exam, no matter what I wrote, I would not receive a grade higher than a 70. Based on this, I studied harder for her examination than for any of my other classes. My study partner and close friend was Frank McClellan. We spent most of the night prior to the exam studying for it. I was determined not to get a grade of less than a 90. When the exam was over, I felt very good about it. My final grade in the class was 72. My study partner Frank earned the highest grade in the class. He would leave Howard after one year due to his disgust with the slowness of the registration procedures and the atmosphere at the school and complete his legal education at Duquesne and Yale law schools. He would go on to distinguish himself in the field of law as a Distinguished Professor at Temple University School of Law and as an outstanding litigator. His co-authored a text book which is used in several law schools entitled: _Tort Law: Cases, Materials, Problems._

Except for these two incidents my other experiences at Howard were rather uneventful. I had the good fortune of having some exceptionally brilliant teachers. Professor Jerome Shuman made the course on Property an exciting adventure into a new realm of knowledge. Judge James Washington, who taught a course on Decedent's Estates

Noel Myricks

was a spellbinding orator with a wealth of knowledge to transmit to his students. The Criminal law and Procedure Professor, who would eventually become Dean of the law school, Paul Miller made this area of the law and our moot court experiences memorable. His reputation as an outstanding Criminal Defense attorney in Washington, D.C., was legendary. We lived a block away from each other and he was also someone I regarded as a personal friend.

One afternoon in a bar near the Howard campus, I engaged him in a discussion about his practice of law. I wanted to know why he quit practicing law. I told him that others had told me about his reputation as an outstanding litigator, and the fees he could command which were substantially more than what he earned as Dean.

He took a drink, looked at me and said, "Noel, if you do your research you will discover that the rate of alcoholism in the legal profession is highest among those who are criminal defense attorneys. When you drive down the street here in D.C., what do you see?" He paused, and then said, "Bars' on the windows and doors. You never know whether that person walking into your office, especially in the evening, is coming to obtain your legal services or coming to rob you because they think that since you are a lawyer, you have some money on you." He died prematurely of Cirrhosis of the liver while taking a nap on the couch in his living room. His young daughter came home from elementary school and tried to wake him to no avail.

Sometimes I Feel Like a Fatherless Child

The Professor that I had for Civil Rights was the former Attorney General of the United States, Ramsey Clark. What more could one ask for?

The Negro National Anthem
"Stony the road we trod, bitter the chast'ning rod

Felt in the days when hope unborn had died;

Yet with the steady beat, have not our weary feet

Come to the place for which our fathers sighed?

We have come over a way that with tears has been watered.

We have come treading our path through the blood of the slaughtered,

Out from the gloomy past, till we stand at last

Where the white gleam of our bright star is cast.

God of our weary years, God of our silent tears,

Thou who has brought us thus far on the way;

Thou who has by Thy might let us into the light

Keep us forever in the path we pray."

Noel Myricks

Life Ev'ry Voice and Sing

James Weldon Johnson

Introduction to the Teaching Profession

Although I had a scholarship, and my wife worked, I wanted to supplement my income with a part-time job. Since I had a Master's degree, I decided to explore teaching opportunities on the campus. After reviewing the Schedule of Classes on the campus, I noticed that a course entitled *"Argumentation and Debate"* did not have anyone listed to teach it. My debate course had been my most enjoyable course at San Francisco State. I went to the Department of Speech and talked to the Chairman of the Department about my interest and qualifications, and to my pleasant surprise he hired me not only as the instructor for the course but also as the Director of Debate.

Although I did not know it at the time, this event would greatly influence my career plans. I thoroughly enjoyed my experiences in these positions. A very good debate program was developed and I took enormous pride in the success of my teams in intercollegiate debate competition. I was especially delighted to have my top debater, *Rosezella Canty* be selected as one of 10 debate students selected nationally to represent the United States Debate Team in a tour of the British Isles. Rosezella would go on to earn a law degree from Harvard. Teaching debate classes proved to be one of my most enjoyable experiences at Howard.

It was through experiences of this kind that I became familiar with other segments of the campus community. One of my debaters, *Calvin McDowell* introduced me to a friend. She was a beautiful young lady who aspired to become a professional dancer and/or actress – *Debbie Allen*. She has gone on to become an internationally recognized director, choreographer and author; A member of the American Film Institute and the recipient of three *Emmy* awards and one *Golden Globe* and also the recipient of numerous other honors.

My second year of law school also proved to be quite eventful. In March 1968 the administration building on campus was seized by students demanding campus reform and a Black-oriented curriculum. Protests at the law school were initiated primarily by some members of my class and the result was the ouster of the newly appointed Dean, *Patricia Roberts Harris*. The popular choice to replace her was Professor *Paul Miller*. Shortly thereafter, Professor Harris resigned and left the university. Within a year, the President of the University, *James Nabrit* would retire and be replaced by Dr. James Cheek who would offer a new vision for the university. The campus, like the country was experiencing its convulsions.

When my second year came to an end, I took two law courses during the summer at the American University. One was Consumer Protection Law and the other one was Civil Rights and Liberties. The professor who taught the Consumer Protection law course was employed full-time at Howard. I had him for Commercial Law at Howard and received a grade of "66." At AU, I missed earning a grade of "A" from him by one point. He asked me afterwards how I accounted for such a discrepancy in my performance. My response was that I could only explain it on the atmosphere and how it affected my motivation. I earned the grade of "A" in the Civil Rights and Liberties course.

When the fall semester began, I interviewed for a full-time teaching position at a new academic institution – The Federal City College even though still attending law school. I was hired to teach courses on Counseling and a course on Poverty and the Law in the Department of Urban Studies. I looked forward to this new challenge as I approached my third and final year of law school.

My most challenging courses in law school were behind me. There was only one third year course that caused students considerable apprehension including me. It was Federal Jurisdiction. There were two sections. One was taught by *Oliver "Red" Morse*, a highly respected scholar with exceptional analytical, communication and interpersonal skills. The other section was taught by Elwood "Chick" Chisolm.

When I learned that I had been scheduled to attend the section taught by Professor Chisolm, I used every conceivable tactic and contact imaginable to avoid this, and I was not alone in my efforts; several other students did the same thing. During my two years there, I knew that too many students ahead of me had mistakenly assumed they were going to graduate, but found out otherwise when they received their final course grade in Federal Jurisdiction from Professor Chisolm. I did not want to be one of them.

One student who had learned to his dismay that he had not successfully passed this course came to Professor Chisolm with tears in his eyes. He asked Professor Chisolm to give him another opportunity to pass the examination. He told the professor that his parents had sent invitations to other family members and friends, and they would be coming to see him graduate. His words fell on deaf ears. He offered to do additional work for extra credit; all he needed was a grade of "D" in the course and he could graduate. Professor Chisolm was unsympathetic to his pleas.

As a final act of desperation, the student pulled out a gun and pointed it at the professor and told him that if he did not give him another chance to pass the examination or give him a grade of "D" he would kill him. Professor Chisolm looked at him and purportedly uttered a few short expletives and said, "Pull the trigger or get the [expletive] out of my office." The student, completely devastated broke down and cried even more profusely—he put the gun away and hurriedly left his office. Professor Chisolm called the police and had him arrested.

I did not need any more headaches from Professor Chisolm at that point in my life. Hence, I was quite pleased to learn that permission had been granted for me to take Federal Jurisdiction from Professor Morse which I successfully passed.

Powell v. McCormick

While in law school, I went to the U.S. Supreme Court to hear Adam Clayton Powell's case argued before the Court. He had been elected to the House of Representatives for the 90th Congress. Although he met the age, citizenship and residence requirements enumerated in the U.S. Constitution, Powell was not permitted to take his seat pursuant to a House Resolution after a Select Committee of the House reported that Congressman Powell "had asserted an unwarranted privilege and immunity from the processes of the courts of New York; that he had wrongfully diverted House funds for the use of others and himself; and that he had made false reports on expenditures of foreign currency to the Committee on House Administration.

Congressman Powell sought a federal declaration that his exclusion was unconstitutional, and that his salary should be paid. The lower courts had dismissed his Complaint.

The U.S. Supreme Court, with Chief Justice Earl Warren rendering the opinion ruled that the House of Representatives may not exclude a duly elected representative who meets the constitutionally defined requirements for membership. In essence, the House could not arbitrarily exclude a member of the House who met the constitutional requirements to serve in Congress.

This case was argued by my Constitutional law professor, *Herbert O. Reid* and Professor *Arthur Kinoy* of Rutgers University. Their oral advocacy was quite impressive. What I found particularly impressive was their refutation of the pre-Constitutional Convention precedents of the English Parliament and American Colonial Assemblies, the debates at the Constitutional Convention and State Conventions as well as the early and more recent Congressional precedents that opposing counsel tried to use to support the view that the House had a "judicially unreviewable power to set qualifications for membership and to judge whether prospective members me those qualifications."

Professor Kinoy was particularly impressive as he pointed out in great detail how opposing counsel was relying on precedents that had not been adopted after the enactment of the U.S. Constitution. He emphasized the Hamiltonian principle which he described as fundamental to our representative democracy – "that the people should choose whom they please to govern them." The mere act of being present to hear the arguments provided an education itself.

Noel Myricks

Federal City College

My first year at the Federal City College was an enjoyable one. There was a feeling that faculty members were in a position to create a whole new educational institution that would be more sensitive and responsive to the human needs of its students and the residents of the District of Columbia. We believed that we were limited only by our imagination.

Department and Division Chairpersons were elected by the faculty and not appointed by the President. This seemed ideal at the time, however, without control of our budgets, it would present problems in the future that none of us had anticipated.

By the end of my first year I had graduated from law school and managed to get elected as Chair of the Department of Urban Studies in the Division of Social Sciences. My plans to return to California and join the law firm of then Assemblyman Willie Brown changed. I enjoyed what I was doing and there had been a substantial increase in my income. I hypothesized that if I returned to California I would have to take a substantial decrease in income before I had become established in the practice of law. I decided that I was not prepared to make such a financial sacrifice. Although I did not know it at the time, financially speaking, this would prove to be a huge mistake on my part.

Willie would become one of the most politically influential people in the State of California. Those who were members of his law firm had their careers enhanced. As one of them told me after becoming a Judge: "Noel, you should have returned and joined us."

One of my former law school classmates, *Billy Hunter*, who I saw at the White House when *Jimmy Carter* was President told me he had taken my advice and gone to California and cultivated a relationship with *Willie Brown* and *Dr. Carlton Goodlett*, my former Physician, who was the Editor and Owner of the San Francisco Sun Reporter, the most influential black newspaper in the bay area. He said they were very instrumental in him becoming the U.S. Attorney for Northern California. He subsequently became the Executive Director of the National Basketball Players Association, with a salary in excess of a million dollars a year.

As a new developing institution, the Federal City College had its various interest groups among the faculty and the administration. Each group was trying to establish its own power base. Some of the students attending and active in student government were inmates at Lorton Penitentiary. They had been allowed to attend classes at the college under a special program between the college and the government of the District of Columbia. These students and other students in the student government appeared to be closely aligned to some members in the Administration. Thus when there were major disagreements between the direction that the faculty wanted to go and one that the administration wanted to pursue, there would be veiled threats of physical harm by these students.

When tension arose between the faculty in the Social Sciences Division and the Administration, a meeting was arranged with the President. When one of the faculty members, who had been the former Provost tried to find common ground for a resolution of our differences so that we could work together in a more cooperative and collaborative way, one of the students present began to loudly berate and verbally abuse and physically threaten her. When the Division Chairperson asked the President what he was going to do about such abusive behavior, the President remarked that students had the right to exercise their freedom of speech just like everyone else. Shortly thereafter the meeting was adjourned when it became apparent that nothing constructive would be accomplished.

When we returned to our offices, the Division Chairperson decided to tender his resignation. He stated that he did not feel that he could function any longer in an atmosphere of intimidation. A group of faculty members decided that we would have a private meeting at a colleague's house and decide who we would support to replace him.

Two factions were present at this meeting. Small cadres of the faculty members present were perceived as being aligned with the administration. The majority felt alienated by the administration. Two persons were nominated; one from each faction. The candidate that I and the majority of persons supported prevailed. Congratulations were extended and a discussion about the direction the Division should take in the current atmosphere became the topic for discussion. The losing candidate, Edward Marksman, leaned over and whispered to the winner to accompany him and a friend to another part of the house so that they could talk alone; ostensibly, to mend fence. The three got up and went into an adjacent bedroom.

Approximately five minutes later, I decided to use the restroom. As I walked past the bedroom where the three were, I observed our newly elected Chairperson on his knees being badly beaten and kicked by *Edward Marksman* while his crony was hitting our Chairman in the head with his African walking stick. I rushed back to the living room and got assistance from others to intervene. Everyone rushed to the rescue.

The police and an ambulance had to be called. Amazingly, the police tried to get us not to press charges. Our Chairman had to be taken to the hospital where he remained for quite a while with some serious injuries. Criminal and civil charges were brought against the two faculty members who retained one of the best criminal defense attorneys in Washington, D.C. Both were suspended from the institution subject to the outcome of the criminal trial. Virtually everyone not involved in the altercation was astonished to learn that the two assailants had only been charged with Assault. It was the considered opinion of many of us that the Chairman would have been killed or seriously maimed if intervention had not occurred.

I had learned enough from my criminal law class to know that the odds would be substantial that a relatively inexperienced prosecutor would, in all likelihood, be assigned to prosecute this case given the nature of the charge. If so, I believed that the ends of justice would not be served. I took the initiative to go see my trial advocacy professor, Luke Moore, the Chief Prosecutor for the District of Columbia. He was popular with his students and we had given him the nickname *Cool Hand Luke* because of his demeanor, manner of speech and the way he handled himself. He had an outstanding record as a prosecutor and was the top gun in the office of the prosecutor.

I pleaded with him to prosecute this case himself and not allow someone with less experience to handle it. I emphasized the importance of the case and the message that it would send to other hoodlums if these thugs were found not guilty. He agreed to do so.

Ordinarily, a trial of this nature would not have lasted longer than a day. However, with these two superb adversaries, the trial lasted three days and then a verdict was rendered – Guilty!

Luke Moore, who eventually became a judge, was the only man to whom I have ever sent flowers. He deserved all the accolades for an outstanding performance in this trial. If there had been an attorney of lesser ability, I am confident, considering the skill of the defense attorney that the decision would have been not guilty.

Edwin A. Marksman, Jr., along with his partner lost their jobs and had to pay substantial damages in a civil suit. Marksman subsequently relocated to Chicago where he taught briefly for the University of Illinois. A few years later he was stabbed to death by muggers. He had been trained in the martial arts and decided that he could resist being robbed. This incident was reported in *Jet* Magazine.

Tension between the faculty and the administration increased. The newly elected Chair who had been beaten resigned and I was selected to replace him. Although no one had threatened me, I was keenly aware of the fact that some students attending were prison inmates. I became so concerned about my own physical well-being that I decided to carry a gun to work that I had purchased during the time I worked as a Deputy Sheriff. Based on what I saw happen to the former Chair, I decided that if someone attacked me while I walked to my car at night which was located in a parking lot behind the building, I would send them to meet their Maker. I was determined not to allow anyone to brutalize me as they had done to one of my predecessors.

The time came when I decided that I could not walk the tightrope between the demands of the faculty and those of the administration. As I got ready to put my .38 Smith & Wesson into my briefcase one day, I paused and asked myself: "What in the heck am I doing? Who needs this?" At that point I decided to leave the Federal City College.

American University

Since I had envisioned working in higher education, I decided to pursue a doctorate degree in Higher Education from the American University while completing my third year of law school and working at the Federal City College. I took my transcript to AU to get an informal evaluation of it and to determine, how much, if any of the credits I had received at San Francisco State would be accepted toward their doctoral requirement of 72 hours.

I met with a professor in the Department of Education, who after reviewing my transcript and my Board score stated that AU would accept 30 of the 60 graduate hours I had earned at SFSC. He also stated that my Board scores on the Miller Analogies would be the second highest of those students entering the doctoral program in the fall. I asked, out of curiosity, who had the highest score. The professor stated that distinction belonged to a retired Admiral who had done his undergraduate work at the U.S. Naval Academy. I said that as a former navy enlisted man, I had no problem deferring to the Admiral.

Shortly after submitting my formal application for admission, I received a letter of rejection. Of course, that took me by surprise. I telephoned the Chairman of the

Education Department, who had signed off on the letter to inquire why I was rejected. He surprised me further by stating that my Board scores were too low. My response to that comment was that I found his statement interesting since I had an informal evaluation of my credentials before I applied, and I was informed that I would have the second highest score of persons' entering the program in the Fall.

The Chairman began to stutter. It was obvious that he had not known this. I told him that I was coming to the university within the hour, with my official scores from the Princeton Board, and I would like to compare these scores with the ones he used to reject me.

Upon arriving on campus, I promptly went to the office of the Chairman, greeted him and asked to see my scores. He pulled a manila folder out of his files and showed me scores that had been handwritten inside the folder. I reviewed them and told him those were not my scores, and then I produced an official copy from the Board. When he saw them he had difficulty looking me in the eye, and he became very incoherent trying to explain the handwritten scores.

Finally, he spoke, "These scores will certainly get you in; in fact, you are admitted now."

Shortly thereafter, I went to the Office of Financial Aid. I was greeted there by someone with the title *Colonel*. For the sake of this discussion, he will be called *"Colonel Sanders*."* Even though I was now accepted by the university, the tuition was $100.00 per credit hour, and I could not afford to pay that. I told the Colonel that I came to get a National Defense Fellowship. He asked me a few questions, and upon learning that I was going to be a doctoral student, he informed me that I had applied too late, and the only money they had left was for persons' who would be pursuing the Bachelor's degree.

I told the Colonel that it was not my fault that I had applied late; that this problem was caused by a person in the Department of Education, and further, the legislative intent of the National Defense Education Act was that priority was to be given to those pursuing the doctoral degree who planned to teach; not those who were pursuing a Bachelor's degree.

He said, "Mr. Myricks, I'm sorry, but we simply do not have any money for you; we have to give priority to our undergraduate students."

At this point, I looked at him and said in a very calm and deliberate voice, "Colonel Sanders, I'm in my last year of law school at Howard. I do not want you to misconstrue what I'm about to say; I am not threatening you, but simply informing you of what I plan to do when I leave here. I'm going home and draft a complaint and sue the American University and you. And the moment I file this suit, I'm going to subpoena your financial aid records and require you to identify, in discovery, the race of each recipient of financial aid for the past five years and the amount received. If I can detect a racial disparity in the allocation of funds, I will then proceed to get the federal government to terminate all financial aid to AU. You have a good day Sir."

Predictably, by the time I got home, and as I was reaching for my door knob, my phone was ringing incessantly. When I picked it up I heard a voice with a heavy southern drawl on the other end say, "Mr. Myricks, this is Colonel Sanders, we found some money for you; we found some money for you. When can you come back?"

To make a long story short, I spent less than a hundred dollars to earn a doctoral degree from the American University, and that money was spent either in the cafeteria or bookstore. For a while, it got embarrassing. One Financial Aid Assistant, upon observing me walk down the hall would almost jump out of her seat and come into the hall and ask me if I needed any more money, and if I did, whatever I needed was forthcoming.

The bottom line that this lesson should teach is that if people are not willing to fight for what they want, they deserve what they get.

University of Maryland

While attending a Bar Review course I met a Provost at the College Park campus of the University of Maryland. She asked whether I would be interested in coming to College Park, and when I responded in the affirmative, she arranged an interview for me with the Chair of the Department of Family and Community Development.

After meeting with him and other faculty members, I was hired at Maryland in the fall of 1972.

I purchased my first house, a beautiful one, in the planned community of Columbia, Maryland in 1972. Any thoughts that I entertained about returning to California vanished. I was also earning as much money through various consulting opportunities as I earned in salary. The pressures that I had experienced at the Federal City College were non-existent at the University of Maryland.

Although Maryland was far from perfect, the atmosphere, especially in my department was relaxed and congenial. I taught courses on Family Law, Children in the Legal System, Family Crises and Rehabilitation, Program Planning and Needs Assessment, Family Mediation and on occasion courses in the Department of Kinesiology on Amateur Sports law and Professional Sports law. I supervised students doing Master's theses and doctoral dissertations. These experiences enabled me to draw heavily on my interdisciplinary background. I also wrote a draft proposal for what eventually became the *Center on Aging*.

When Jimmy Carter was elected President of the United States, I was appointed by him to be on the National Advisory Council on Extension and Continuing Education. This provided me with the opportunity to contribute to federal policy in this area. I also received several invitations to social gatherings at The White House.

Maryland also gave me the opportunity to develop an intercollegiate mock trial team. After considerable success in mock trial, I was given the privilege of selecting two students who I could train and take to *Melbourne, Australia* to compete in the World *British Parliamentary Debate Tournament*. The students selected were female and male; white and black, graduate and undergraduate, U.S. and foreign nationalities. Both were students with outstanding academic credentials who distinguished themselves at this tournament. I became quite comfortable in my roles at Maryland.

My outside interests included working as a trial attorney, a grievance examiner for the National Institutes of Health, a Mediator and Case Evaluator in both civil and domestic relations for the Superior Court of the District of Columbia and an investigator of EEO discrimination complaints filed by federal employees against other federal personnel in federal agencies.

Two of the more interesting experiences I had while working as a part-time counselor occurred at a half-way house for juveniles in the District of Columbia. A doctoral student in the School of Social Work at Howard had previously held the position but he resigned when his life was threatened. I did not know this until after I had accepted the job.

The ages of those in this half-way house varied from 16-18. One young black male there stood out from the others because of his personal appearance and manners. His appearance was immaculate and his manners were impeccable. He seemed completely out-of-place. When I asked him why he was here, he said he had been arrested for armed robbery and attempted murder. He said that he had tried to rob a bank and a security guard behind him told him to drop his weapon, and he turned and quickly fired in the direction of the voice.

He missed his target and was apprehended. I was still inclined to give him the benefit of the doubt, thinking that perhaps he simply wanted to scare the guard. I said, "But you really didn't mean to kill him did you?"

To my surprise, he said, "yes, because he could identify me."

I looked at him and walked away thinking about how one's appearance can be deceiving.

When I returned for my third counseling session with the group, one of the young men who appeared to be the toughest member and leader of the group said at the outset of the counseling session that he didn't like me and if I showed up again, he would kill me. Like some of the others, he had been incarcerated for various assault charges and attempted murder, and he was the one who had scared away my predecessor.

The group present was comprised of approximately 10-12 persons. Based on my background, I knew that I had two options:

(1) resign

(2) Confront him.

I chose the latter. I told him that he did not know me nor did he know my background. I said as a young man, I was a very good fighter and when I got older I worked as a Correctional Officer at San Quentin and during my first week witnessed a man killed in its gas chamber, and I had also worked as a Deputy Sheriff for the City and County of San Francisco, and I still had my guns from that job, and when I returned, and I would return, I will be ready for any attempt on my life.

He looked at me in a threatening manner, and then I said, if you want to take me on now, make your move and I will take this television that I am sitting next to and bust you in your head with it and wrap it around your neck. So feel free to make your move at anytime. Neither he nor anyone else said anything. I conducted the counseling session and afterwards reported this incident to the Supervisor of the house. When I returned the following week, he had been sent back to jail because of the threat.

In addition to my teaching responsibilities at Maryland, I would advise students on careers and prep courses that had proven successful for admission to law or graduate school and I would lobby members of admission committees at various institutions for a student's admission. I knew, based on my experiences as a student, that students need advice; advice about such things as the right courses to take; how much time to spend on their homework or extracurricular activities and the importance of finding a faculty mentor or teacher and the questions to ask them. In essence, get to know your teachers.

I thoroughly enjoyed teaching and the mentoring of students. Teaching enabled me to draw not only on my interdisciplinary background, but also my life experiences. Based on my experiences at the University of San Francisco, I knew that one's success in college could depend, to a great extent on excellent counseling, advising and mentoring.

Mentoring provides a person with an opportunity to have a positive impact on another person's life. When I served as a mentor, I tried to enable students to get the benefit of over a half century of living a full life.

I would try to get insight into who the person is and what were his or her dreams. What in essence was the person's self-concept and how I could impact on this person in a very positive and constructive way. I would obtain background information (family history, academic success or lack of success, aspirations, specifically what would the person like to achieve in life).

Occasionally, depending on our rapport with each other, and whether I felt it would be useful, I would share my own life experiences, i.e., a child born out of wedlock, raised on welfare, received good grades in elementary and high school only in music and physical education, military experiences and the value of travel and widening one's knowledge about the world and how at least one former teacher admitted that he thought I would be dead or in prison before I ever got out of high school. Those with whom I shared such personal information, more often than not were, to say the least, surprised.

One young man, a basketball player had become academically ineligible to play basketball, and his coach sent him to me to see what, if any assistance I could provide him to get his life together. I quickly concluded that the counseling and guidance that he had received had not served him well. I advised him to change his major to one that I believed was more suitable for him. He was also required to come to my office so that I could monitor his progress in all his courses.

He saw a picture of *Len Bias* on my desk. Len was arguably the finest basketball player to come out of Maryland. I told him that I had talked to Len the day before he died. I had congratulated Len on being drafted by the Boston Celtics, and warned him about the perils of drugs and other things.

Len's last words to me were, "I got everything together Professor Myricks; I got it together, I'm not going to mess up."

The following day when I arrived at my office, a colleague notified me that Len was dead. I told this student that he had a responsibility, not only to himself, but his family and his people, and to do anything less than his very best, was a disservice to them. I told him that I did not go to Len's funeral because I was angry that he had lied to me and wasted his life, and I hoped he would not do the same.

This student and I would spend three to four hours once or twice a week for a year. When he made the Athletic Director's Dean's List, which recognizes athletes who achieve a 3.0 or above grade point average at the end of the year, he said that it was the greatest moment in his academic life. He went on to graduate from Maryland and have a long career in the National Basketball Association. He described me as his "second father." He also made a nice contribution to my endowed scholarship fund for students whose parents had never attended college upon my retirement.

On another occasion, I recall a young female student who had two classes from me during the same semester: Family Law and Children in the Legal System. She always came to class thoroughly prepared and by the end of the semester had earned a grade of "A" in oral participation. And then there were final examinations.

Her final examinations were on two consecutive days. After her first examination, before I left that day, the examinations were graded and she had received an "F". When she came to class the following day, I did not say anything to her until she came to my desk to turn in her examination. When she did I asked her to wait until others left, there was something I wanted to discuss with her. When other students left the room, I told her the grade she had earned on her first examination. She immediately broke down and began to cry. After she calmed down, I told her there was too much of a discrepancy between my evaluation of her performance throughout the semester and what she did on the final examination. I also told her that I would not look at her second examination until my hypothesis had been tested. I sent her over to the Counseling Center to be examined, and my hypothesis was confirmed. She had dyslexia, which is a serious learning disability and which makes reading, writing and spelling impaired.

She subsequently took her examinations again at the Counseling Center, with that situation addressed and received final grades of "A" and "B." Her parents came to see me to express their appreciation for detecting this. They wanted to know how she could have gone so long through high school and college without anyone detecting it. I told them that I could not answer that question, but my background in psychology and rehabilitation counseling was helpful.

As time passed, I attracted students from various departments across the campus. One young man, an engineering student who went on to become an Intellectual Property Attorney wrote after becoming a member of the Bar:

"You were the most powerful force in my career as an undergraduate at College Park. I always refer to you as my advisor even though you're in Family Studies instead of the mechanical engineering department. When I did not get accepted into Franklin Pierce Law Center, you suggested that I call them and arrange an interview. Per your advice, I did this.

Noel Myricks

After the interview, I was accepted. I never thanked you while I was in college. Thank you very much for pushing me while I was in college and suggesting the field of law. If it weren't for you, I would not have considered law, gained acceptance to law school and eventually become a member of the bar. I will be indebted to you for many years to come."

Letters such as this are representative of the numerous letters that I have received from former students. Another former student and Harvard law graduate said,

"Dr. Myricks has had an extraordinary impact on his students. Many who had no expectation of going to graduate school or even an expectation that they would graduate from college find their entire belief system transformed by him. They complete honors theses when they never thought that anyone would care to read what they wrote. They seek doctorates when they earlier planned to drop out. Dr. Myricks inspires us, moves us and guides us because he cares about us. Dr. Myricks expects more from undergraduate students than anyone may have expected from them in their entire lives – often more than they even expect from themselves."

The Family Law course that I taught at Maryland had an advocacy component where in addition to learning the Case Method, students had to engage in cross-examination debate on a timely Family Law topic. One day a colleague who was an Assistant Dean in the College of Liberal Arts gave me a flier about intercollegiate mock trial competition. He thought this might be something in which I would be interested.

Upon further investigation I discovered that the program was based in Des Moines, Iowa and had approximately 200 colleges and universities from around the country competing, including those from the Ivy League as well as Berkeley, Stanford, Northwestern and Chicago.

A program was developed at Maryland and during our third year of competition, Maryland's two teams finished first and second in the nation, which was unprecedented.

As a result of our success, the American Mock Trial Association developed what became known as *The Maryland Rule.* This rule precluded teams from the same institution from ever being able to compete against each other again. By the end of the decade, the Association had named Maryland *the Mock Trial Team of the Nineties.*

By the time I retired, Maryland had won four national championships, a Gold Flight championship and 11 regional championships. The response from the university, the State legislature and the Governor was replete with accolades and awards. An endowed scholarship was created in my name and I had been the recipient of numerous Outstanding Teacher and Mentor awards. When I concluded my career at the University of Maryland, I had the satisfaction of knowing that I had made a positive difference in the lives of many students and enabled them to achieve what may have been at some point in time an unthinkable dream.

Based on my background and the absence of a father, I tried to be very involved in my son's life. I was a firm believer that if you could handle yourself physically, that would give you the confidence in your ability to achieve in other areas. Thus, my son became a Black Belt in Tae Kwon do at the age of 13. When he graduated from high school, he was accepted for admission to the Massachusetts Institute of Technology and graduated with a degree in Electrical Engineering. He went on to earn two law degrees and a graduate degree in Electrical Engineering and became an Intellectual Property Attorney.

There also came a time while teaching at Maryland that I went to an ice cream parlor near the campus to relax and enjoy the ice cream. As I sat down I observed two former students waving at me from another booth. I responded in kind and decided to join them. They introduced me to their sister who was with them. I found her enormously appealing. She seemed fixated on the strawberry stripe sundae she had in front of her. Nonetheless, we talked and became friends. As time passed, I became not only her friend, but her mentor and eventually her husband and law partner. Some long-time friends described her as my "trophy-wife." We had 14 years of a wonderful marriage. We traveled to the Caribbean, Australia and Europe. On one occasion we took an entire month and spent a week in Paris, two weeks on the French Riviera and divided a week between Rome, Barcelona, and Palma de Mallorca. While in Australia my wife conceived our only child, a daughter whom I named after my mother – Mollie.

During our marriage, my wife became one of *Jehovah's Witnesses*. Periodically, I would attend her place of worship with her. And then one day she began to complain about a pain below her right lower rib cage. When she went to the doctor at our HMO she was told that she had a virus and was given some antibiotics. When the pain did not go away she returned and her doctor panicked because she realized that she had misdiagnosed her. Further tests revealed that my wife had breast cancer and it had metastasized and she was given a prognosis of no more than three months to live. We were devastated. At that time our daughter was one month shy of being four years old.

As the end drew near my wife was hospitalized at Georgetown University Hospital. I would often stay with her around the clock, with her father coming to give me time to go home, shower, and get some sleep and return. As death approached, I said to her, "I'm puzzled about something. You are in a lot of pain and we both know your prognosis. During all of this, I have never seen one tear come from your eyes. I've known guys; tough guys, who have gone into a fetal position crying, fearful of death. I have not seen any fear or remorse in you."

She looked at me and said, "I know what is waiting on me Noel so I have no fear. If you continue studying, you will know what I know. I do not want you to become one of Jehovah's Witnesses because you think it is something that I want you to do. You have to want it for yourself. However, I do want you to promise me one thing – that you will raise our daughter as one of Jehovah's Witnesses."

I promised to do that.

Two days later when her father arrived that morning to replace me, I kissed her goodbye and went home to sleep. I picked up our daughter from the babysitter and dozed off. Shortly thereafter my wife's sister called and said that her father had called and told her to call me and tell me to come to the hospital right away. I assumed that my wife's condition had worsened. I took our daughter to the babysitter and rushed to the hospital. When I entered her room, I looked at her and said to her father that she seemed to be sleeping peacefully.

He looked at me and said, "She's gone Noel."

I was devastated. Even though I knew death was near, I still was not prepared to lose her. I rushed to another room and began crying like a baby. A hole was in my heart that I knew could never be repaired. Eventually, when I regained my composure, I returned to her room to look at her and kiss her goodbye. Her father said, shortly before she died, she asked him to help her get out of bed and to put her pillow on the floor so she could put her knees on it and pray. He did this and then she got back in bed, with his assistance, shut her eyes and began to hum *Kingdom Melody* songs. And then she was gone forever. This was August 22, 1998.

I kept my promise to her about our daughter. I was baptized as one of Jehovah's Witnesses in 2002. I had come to understand what my wife meant when she told me that if I continued to study I would learn what she already knew. Namely, because of the resurrection, we do not need to have a morbid fear of death. Christians have found that the resurrection hope is a source of strength beyond what is normal when they undergo trials that bring them face-to-face with death. Our daughter, at the age of 13 was baptized in 2007.

I married again in 2003. The woman I married, *Kimberly* and her family had been close friends of my family. They are also Jehovah's Witnesses. Even before my former wife died, they had been very supportive of us during her illness. When she died, their support continued. I found Kimberly to be a very attractive and a spiritually strong person and a woman who would be an excellent wife and mother. Within three months after our marriage, my daughter Mollie informed us that she wanted Kimberly to adopt her. Kimberly eagerly agreed to do so and shortly thereafter I went to court and filed the adoption papers.

The two of them always had a close relationship. On occasion, prior to the time we were married, Mollie would spend the night at Kimberly's house, and Kimberly would take her to various places and interact with her as one might expect a mother to interact with her child. They had bonded and become inseparable. Sometimes I had to wonder if they were locked at the hip.

Later that year I became ill after coming home from work. I became feverish and began experiencing severe pain on my right side. I also experienced nausea and commenced vomiting and could not eat for 24 hours. Eventually, I had to be taken to the hospital emergency room. Although various tests were conducted, I was misdiagnosed as having a virus and sent home.

Within 24 hours after returning home, my condition became worse and I had to return to the hospital. Based on the fact that my wife had experienced similar symptoms several years before, she suggested to the attending physician that she thought it was my gall bladder. The attending physician looked at her as though she did not have the credentials to make such a diagnosis and dismissed her suggestion.

My wife asked for a second opinion and specifically requested that *Dr. Peter LeNard*, who was not affiliated with the hospital, be asked to come in for a consultation. Reluctantly, the attending physician agreed. When Dr. LeNard arrived at approximately 10:p.m. he examined me and concluded that my problem was the gall bladder and surgery should be performed immediately.

When the surgery was performed it was discovered that not only had the gall bladder stopped functioning, but it was gangrene. I was sent home shortly after the operation. Within 24 hours, I began experiencing extreme abdominal pain. My wife called 911. When they arrived I had to be carried down the steps of my house to the ambulance and taken back to the hospital.

It was discovered that my body was retaining fluid and I couldn't urinate. I had to be catheterized again to drain fluids. Soon thereafter I was told that I would be discharged to return home. Eventually, my wife was told she could help me dress to take me home. When she felt my back while dressing me, she detected that I had a fever. She went to the nurses' station and demanded that someone take my vitals because no one had done so prior to the time I was told I could be discharged. My temperature was quite high and at that point my wife demanded that I be admitted to the hospital. She was told that they had no rooms available.

She said, "FIND ONE!"

She told them that if anything happened to me based on their initial misdiagnosis; or releasing me too early which prompted my having to return to the hospital, she would sue and her name would be on the hospital.

This prompted the medical staff to scurry around and find me a private room where I remained for two nights. During this time I was closely monitored and even pampered with a full body aromatic massage. Dr. Lenard returned to monitor my care. When I told him how thankful I was for his attention, he said that it wasn't him but it was my wife who made sure that I received the care I needed. In essence, she had a major role in saving my life, and I am blessed and grateful for her.

Noel Myricks

RETIREMENT

While teaching a summer class, a student came to me at the end of the class and asked how long I had been teaching at Maryland. The question took me somewhat by surprise. I paused and had to count the years because I had never thought about it. Finally, I said "30 years. Why?"

She smiled and said, "I thought so. You taught my mother and she told me to give you her regards."

Although I could not remember her mother I pretended otherwise and told her to tell her mother I said hello. And as I proceeded back to my office, the impact of the student's question caused me to begin thinking about retirement, and within a year I submitted my papers and retired.

As my retirement approached I contemplated my years at the university. I recall that someone once said, *"At the end of your life, you should be able to have pride behind you; love around you and hope in front of you. And if you have this, you have been successful."*

One of the great joys of teaching is to see former students who, when you first met them were uncertain as to whether they would be able to achieve what, at that time, were simply dreams. And then to see them years later and have a tremendous sense of pride knowing that in some small way, you made a contribution to their overall educational development.

When reflecting on my 32 years at Maryland. There were good and bad times, however, the good times clearly outweighed the bad times. I took considerable pride in the fact that several of my former mock trial students had gone to some of the most prestigious law and graduate schools in the country: Yale, Harvard, Stanford, Chicago, Berkeley, Michigan and Georgetown. One young man who had been the best medical "expert" I ever had in mock trial went on to Johns Hopkins Medical School and became a member of its faculty. Some went to the Public Policy graduate programs at Harvard and Berkeley. Two former male students, one who became an attorney and another, an engineer, named their children after me.

One former student became the legal and policy advisor for President Clinton's Initiative on Race and subsequently served as the Deputy Assistant Secretary for Civil Rights in the U.S. Department of Education with responsibility for civil rights legal policy development in education.

There were countless others; students who were not in mock trial, and who lacked confidence in their ability. They were encouraged to be confident and went on to graduate and achieve things that they had not envisioned as being possible. My first student assistant at Maryland made an off-the-cuff remark one day as she prepared to complete her Master's degree.

She said, "People will never know how many students you have motivated and helped graduate who would not have graduated if you had not pushed and encouraged them to do so."

Several attended a retirement party for me and created an endowed scholarship in my name. One student wrote in a comment in my retirement book:

"What truly sets this remarkable professor apart from his peers is his genuine interest in the lives of his students, and the actual difference that he makes as a teacher, mentor and friend. He is a tremendous asset to the University of Maryland."

Another student wrote:

"You went far beyond what anyone would have expected, and I know I owe my acceptance to the law school at Michigan to you. I can never thank you enough, but I will make you proud."

The son of one of this country's richest men said in his graduation speech at Lafayette College in Pennsylvania, where I taught for a year while on sabbatical from Maryland that I was one of the three faculty members on the campus who had the greatest impact on his life during his student years at the college.

As my ideology evolved over the years, I came to the point of view that my students were my future. I tried to profit from all that I had experienced in various educational institutions and life to give them the best that I could provide and hope it was good enough. I take enormous pride in their achievements.

Sometimes I Feel Like a Fatherless Child

A colleague who I taught with for 32 years wrote:

"When evaluating Dr. Myricks role as a mentor at this University, one should be aware of the more subtle components of Dr. Myricks contributions. This is a person who has served as an exemplary role model not only for minority students, but for white students as well. Dr. Myricks requests nothing less than 'the best' from all his students. Quality is what he demands and he sets standards that will prove incalculably valuable for students in their careers and personal lives. His office has always served as a haven for energetic and motivated individuals seeking his guidance and assistance."

C.D. Mote, who was President of the College Park campus of the University at the time of my retirement, wrote:

"As a teacher, mentor and mock trial coach, you have set a high benchmark of outstanding service and commitment. Your plethora of undergraduate teaching awards for your Family law courses is a testament to your quality as a teacher. As a mentor you have excelled. Throughout your career, you have devoted countless hours to advising and mentoring family studies majors, first generation college students, campus athletes, students of color and pre-law students from all disciplines. You brought honor to the campus when you received the University of Maryland Regents Award for Mentorship, recognition that you richly deserved.

Your accomplishments as Director and advisor to the Mock Trial Team are extraordinary. Mock Trial at Maryland owes its reputation to your efforts. And it was clear during the

Noel Myricks

event commemorating Brown v. Board of Education that the team members hold you in the greatest esteem. I know that you must be proud of them as they are of you. The University is indebted to you for the time and energy you gave and the standards of excellence you set for our Mock Trial Team.

An outstanding scholar and teacher, you can and should take pride not just in the many students you educated and nurtured and your well-recognized contributions to the study of family law, but in the very fine university you helped to build. It will be a part of your last legacy as a member of the University faculty."

CONCLUSION

While thinking about my life in general, especially its beginning, I am reminded of the words that come from 1 Corinthians 15:10: *"But by God's undeserved kindness I am what I am. And his undeserved kindness that was toward me did not prove to be in vain, but I labored in excess of them all, yet not I but the undeserved kindness of God that is with me."*

The end of my career at the University of Maryland and my life in general can only be described as a series of peaks and valleys. Fortunately, there were more peaks than valleys. I have achieved more than I or anyone who knew me as a young person could ever have envisioned, and for that I feel blessed.

One lesson I learned rather late in life was that education is about change; changing values that are no longer useful and being absolutely clear what your priorities are and discarding those things you formerly enjoyed in order to achieve your goals and objectives.

Your academic credentials may be impeccable and economically you may be in good shape; but spiritually, will you feel fulfilled? Will you know, in your heart and mind that as you prepare to leave this place called Earth, that you have truly done the very best that you could in trying to be a positive force in the lives of those you met along the way? One of the things that students will rarely, if ever, hear a teacher say, and yet it should be said: Make your spiritual development your top priority and then give the substantive matter taught its due or everything else will be nil.

There are numerous examples where this can be shown. One that immediately comes to mind is Deion Sanders, who has been enshrined in the National Football League Hall of Fame. On the surface he had everything going for him: Handsome, rich, charming, college educated, yet, there was a point where he almost committed suicide because of a void in his life. He discovered that the void was a spiritual one and he addressed it.

I have told students that they were entering college during an era where children were killing children; where too many young people were spending time planning for their funerals rather than planning for their vacation. They were entering college where silly arguments could result in the loss of their life and when the pressure to succeed can be so great and disappointment so profound that an increasing number of young people are taking their own lives when they do not live up to the expectation of others.

I have had the good fortune of living over half a century. As I look around I see so many young persons dying from diseases such as AIDS that were non-existent in my youth or becoming victims of homicide. I have to conclude at this point in my life, especially when I consider how often I was one step from disaster, that,

"But for the Grace of God, there go I."

REFERENCES

DuBois, W.E.B.(1903) <u>The Souls of Black Folk.</u> Bantam Books (New York)

Edes, Gordon. (2009) "Rename Cy Young Award After Satchel Paige. Yahoo Sports Exclusive

Gibran, Kahlil (1923) <u>The Prophet</u>. A Borzoi book published by Alfred A. Knopf, Inc. (New York)

Jet Magazine, Stabbing death of Edwin A. Marksman, Jr. (Dec. 24, 1981)

Johnson, James W. & J.R.(1900) "Lift Every Voice and Sing" A poem and hymnal often called "The Negro National Anthem."

Manor, F.E. (1978) <u>A History of River Rouge, Michigan.</u> (Monroe, MI)

Myrdal, Gunnar (1944). <u>An American Dilemma: The Negro Problem and Modern Democracy</u>. Harper & Bros. (New York)

<u>New World Translation of the Holy Scriptures.</u> (1984) Watchtower Bible and Tract Society of New York, Inc. and International Bible Students Association.

Phillips, J.J., Terry, N.P., Maraist, F.L., McClellan, F.M. (1990) <u>Tort Law: Cases, Materials, Problems.</u> The Michie Company (Virginia)

Robeson, Paul (1958) <u>Here I Stand.</u> Beacon Press. (New York)

"The Steel Grey Stabilizer" (1957, Jan) Time Magazine.

Wolfe, Thomas. (1937) <u>You Can't Go Home Again.</u>

Noel Myricks

<u>LAW CASES</u>

Brown v. Board of Education, 347 U.S. 483 (1954)

Dred Scott v. Sandford, 60 U.S. 393 (1857)

Greene v. Howard University, 412 F2d 1128; 134 U.S. App.D.C. 81 (1969)

Powell v. McCormick, 395 U.S. 486 (1969)

Roe v. Wade, 410 U.S. 113 (1973)

<u>add on's</u>

1) 1st wife – Marti – Married Life + Why End

2) Son – Birth experience + present status

3) Sheriffs deputy – MORE SPECIFICS

4) Relating from youth thru old age – Why

5) UDC – Director of Social Sciences

6) Religious Journey

7) always a Pugalist – H.S & NAVY

8) Most beautiful scenery, lifestyles and Women

9) My young life & the pursuit of "ghetto Value"

* 10) Analysis – What I have discovered

11) Index

<u>accenuated or Removed</u>

1) Highschool fights 45 – 51) One Chapter

2) Naval Service fights

? 3) Interracial Relations – sex.
   who is your audience

4) Typo's – p cover quote · quan quest for
   p 260 – me v. met

? – Self Published

Made in the USA
Middletown, DE
10 June 2020

96960918R00177